CONFESSIONS OF A
TIMID RIDER

HEATHER WALLACE

WATER HORSE PRESS

Publisher

Heather Wallace/Water Horse Press LLC

heather@timidrider.com

Cover photography © Jamie Baldanza

Ordering Information: Quantity sales are available for US trade bookstores and wholesalers. For details, contact the publisher at the address above.

Printed in the United States of America

ISBN 978-1-387-81289-9

First Edition

❀ Created with Vellum

To my incredibly supportive husband and daughters, without whom I would not be here today. Thank you for encouraging me to be everything I was meant to be.

INTRODUCTION

For a long time, I let fear get in my way. I always felt like I was missing something when I stepped away from horses during my teens.

I've come a long way since I took that first step back to horsemanship as an adult. When I say I am a timid rider, it is not because I am scared to ride. Oh no, it is because I am scared to fail. I am scared that I cannot live up to my own expectations. That my insecurities will hold me back. Or that I will let my anxiety be greater than my passion once again and step away, or worse, not try to be the person I want to be. My self-doubt tries to hold me back, but I refuse to give in.

These are the confessions of a timid rider.

PART I

BABY GREENS

1

AMBIVERT

What in the world is an ambivert, you ask? I only recently heard the term and thought to myself, "Well, that just makes sense." An ambivert is someone who has both introverted and extroverted tendencies. Sound confusing? In my case I'm an introvert with extroverted traits, depending on my moods, of course.

Introverted Traits

There are several traits classically associated with being an introvert.

Solitude

I relish alone time. My favorite days are when I'm at home writing or reading with my dogs for company. I get cranky when I have to be around people too often or there is a lot of noise and chatter. There is something inherently draining about social situations. Yes, sometimes this includes my own children. I love them but three daughters generate a lot of noise!

Don't get me wrong, I love people, just in small doses and on my own terms. If I start to get overstimulated, I will make an excuse and leave. I call it giving myself a "time out."

Now, I don't do the Irish Exit like some of my friends, (you know who you are), but I will politely say my goodbyes and flee. No music, no chatter. Just blessed silence.

Often, I feel emotionally and physically exhausted after social events and need time to recharge. As the owner of two businesses, a board member of a non-profit, a wife, a mother, and a dog mom – this is not easy to do.

If I think about all the noise in my life, my head would explode.

Writing

As an introvert I spend a lot of time thinking and needing to quietly process my thoughts and feelings. My mind is constantly moving both creatively and logically, so it can be tough to balance.

I've been writing on and off for many years be it poetry,

journal entries, short stories, or on my blog *Bridle &
Bone* that I started in 2016. Putting my thoughts on
paper helps to serve as an outlet for my emotions and
often lets me vent my frustrations properly without the
side effects my verbal diarrhea can have on my loved
ones.

Close Friends

I tend toward small but tight friendships, and there are
few people who know me truly well. I have a lot of
friends, yes. But I have very few CLOSE friends.
Friends I would call to talk with if I'm upset and can
really let my guard down around. It takes a lot for me to
feel safe to open up to someone completely.

You may find this shocking, but I prefer animals over
people.

Gasp!

Okay, okay. I don't know if this is a classic introvert
trait. Animals have a way of giving without taking or
draining energy. There is a natural balance, and I
don't have to be "on" with them. So, despite the fact
that my mother had severe allergies throughout my
childhood, I still had to be surrounded by animals. I
would find stray kittens or pretend to have horses.
Eventually I had very hypoallergenic pets: a goldfish,
a gecko, a hermit crab, etc., basically anything

without fur or feathers. I've always been drawn to animals.

Extrovert

Here's the other side of the coin because, as a Libra, I always need balance. The most common traits of an extrovert can often be described as chatty, social, friendly, and outgoing. Sometimes I tire of my own solitude and seek out social events even though I tend to be a stay-at-home sort. In college my dorm mates at the University of Delaware would tease me and basically drag me out of the building. Go Blue Hens!

So, I found that it became easier and easier to be social, at least for short periods of time. And while I was out, I would make the most of it and choose to be silly, loud, and usually dance my butt off. Others often viewed me as attention-seeking.

Here is where it gets funny. I have been described as both snobbish, (for being guarded and quiet), AND attention-seeking. Really there is no winning here. I learned to not care what other people thought even though, of course, it got to me occasionally. But my opinion of myself counts more than anything and no one is harder on me than well, me.

As an adult I am now somewhere on the spectrum between introvert and extrovert depending on my mood on any given day. Thus, when I heard the term "ambivert," I thought it was a perfect description. After all, no woman wants to be defined by just one thing, right?

Being an ambivert has a lot to do with how I see myself and my riding on any given day. Sometimes I seek the quiet morning when I have the entire barn to myself, but other days I crave the noise and social aspect with my barn friends.

2

THE GRAY PONY INCIDENT

My first time independently on a horse was…interesting.

I was what you would call a horse-obsessed child. Shocking, I know. Instead of imaginary friends I had an imaginary barn full of horses in my backyard. I dreamed of owning a barn one day and breeding Arabians because they were the most beautiful horses I could dream of at the time. I had stuffed horses, Breyer horses, and read as many fiction and non-fiction horse books as I could get my hands on. Obsessed? Perhaps, but I prefer extremely passionate.

There is something inherently noble and graceful about horses. The fact that they trust humans and allow us to share their lives, is a never-ending blessing for me. We all have something we feel connected to, and for me it has always been horses.

I begged to do pony rides at every local circus, party, or event I attended as a child. My parents would shake their heads and laugh, but it was so exciting for me!

However, my first independent experience on horseback didn't go the way I'd dreamed and planned. In fact, it didn't really go at all.

Family vacations should be filled with wonderful memories and they usually are quite memorable for one reason or another. The petty family squabbles or sisterly bickering takes a back seat to the new and amazing experiences. You mostly remember the good times which is a trick our brains play on us so that we do it again and again.

So goes our family trip to Arizona when I was about nine years old. I can still see the dust kicking up as our rental car pulled into the stable yard. My young brain did not take into account the details of the landscape, or the wooden sign marked "Trail Rides." Oh no, the anticipation of riding a horse in the desert was all that I could imagine. Finally, my daydreams and backyard imaginings were coming true. I was a cowgirl!

Sadly, the daydream and the reality could not have been farther apart.

Our family experience had a predictable beginning. The barn owner chose our horses based on experience level and temperament. My pestering was the reason for this equestrian experience that the rest of my family had to endure, and I was the first to mount up on my little gray pony. My favorite color! I knew we were meant to be, and I fell a little bit in love.

We stood waiting for the others in the shade of a tree, the flies dancing around us in the shadows. His tail and ears twitched impatiently as they buzzed quickly by, occasionally landing on me. I was in my glory. My little sister mounted behind us on a dark colored horse, perhaps black or bay. She was nervous. I can still picture it now. She didn't feel comfortable around horses, but she wanted to be like her big sister so she tried to hide her fear. My horse shifted weight as he dozed, and that's when I panicked.

My sudden fear fed my sister's own anxiety. She was following in her sister's footsteps and was taking my lead, trusting that she would be okay. Until I lost my confidence, that is. After all, I was the sister obsessed with horses. My being scared only signaled that there was something to truly be afraid of. The herd mentality at work! I began to imagine that my little gray pony would panic and bolt with me on him, headed off into the vast desert with little old me on his back. I had never ridden independently and did not know my "whoa" from my "go." My fears fed my self-doubt and it became crippling.

So here we were, two little girls sobbing on our ponies in the middle of the Arizona desert. I can only imagine what the other riders were thinking. I'm pretty sure my pony did not budge the entire time despite my wailing. Talk about patient and bombproof! We then dismounted with the help of our guide and then promptly refused to go on the trail. A disappointing beginning for a cowgirl.

My mother stayed with us in the yard while the others went into the desert. My father, a former Air Force Captain and war veteran, had no desire to ride horses. Ironically, he became the only member of our family to venture out that day. He came back a few hours later not wanting to speak about his experience. It was years later that I learned they encountered a rattlesnake on their adventure. He still is wary of horses to this day.

Surprisingly, that day wasn't a total loss. I sat in that dusty Arizona paddock, grooming and loving on that pony, crying when I had to leave. I later realized that I let my fear of what could happen get in the way of something I really wanted to do, and I was disappointed in myself.

In retrospect, I would like to have done things differently and regret not staying on that gray pony and riding off into the desert. I let my fear be greater than my passion and for that reason, a desert ride is still on my equestrian bucket list.

The regret from our Arizona trip has eaten at me for years. My passion for horses didn't waiver; in fact, it grew. But there would always be this niggling doubt that I couldn't handle a horse.

This memory says a lot about me, none of which I'm very proud. I am nothing if not honest with myself and others. I am not embarrassed at the behavior of a young girl who was afraid of riding a strange horse in the Arizona desert. I had no riding experience at all. Zip. Zero. Zilch. My horse didn't misbehave or give me any reason to be scared, but my own insecurities and vivid imagination did that all on its own.

It's a good reminder that one decision can have lasting consequences.

3

SMELLS LIKE TEEN SPIRIT

*S*everal years passed and I managed to convince my parents that I needed to take riding lessons at the local barn. After all, I was much more mature and promised my parents I wouldn't panic again.

While I was born on the West coast, I actually grew up in the wilds of suburban New Jersey. I know, I know, the mythical garbage dump of "New Jersey." Don't pay any attention to the stereotype or what you think you know from watching the Jersey Shore on MTV. Ugh, I still shiver. That show did us no favors in the world.

I grew up in an affluent town in Central New Jersey. There were no farms and not much green space to think of like I have now. But nearby was the Watchung Reservation, a 2,000 acre nature preserve. The reservation is home to Watchung Stables, which has been in operation since 1933 and is where I first became an equestrian.

Lessons were very well organized. Upon arrival I would check the sheet to see what horse I would ride in that day's lesson. Often, they'd been used for a previous lesson and I would ask the rider if there was anything I needed to know about the horse's behavior that day. Horses were tacked and waiting in their stalls so grooming was unnecessary. At the mounting blocks a groom would check my girth and adjust my stirrups as needed. Then I would walk forward and wait in line until the entire class was assembled before proceeding into the ring. All riders would enter and leave the ring en masse. Nice and tidy.

I still remember my first lesson horse who was an older mare named Maizy. She was dead quiet and helped to build my confidence as a new rider. Confidence has always been the thing that got in my way. I always had this fear that I was not good enough, that my horse would bolt, or that I would get hurt. But I loved horses so much that I kept going.

Riding at Watchung Stables as a teenager was a lot of fun. There were some amazing things about the program. Horses were groomed and tacked prior to my arrival, and lessons always began on time. Nearby there where scenic trails to stretch our legs and have an adventure. We often switched horses, so I learned to ride and work with many different personalities.

The downside was that I never learned basic horsemanship. Sometimes a well-oiled machine is a little too well run. I did not know the basics of grooming or cleaning tack. Heck, I didn't even know how to put on a bridle or saddle. Adjusting my stirrups or girth while mounted, never. Grooms did it for me, so I never learned.

I was taught to ride a horse, but I never learned how to be a true horsewoman.

The Wind in My Hair

2,000 acres of nature preserve just down the bridle path from the stable meant amazing trail rides. These are still my favorite things about riding. The fog would blanket the paddocks, showing glimpses of deer grazing alongside their hooved brethren. As we walked toward the trailhead, the deer would turn and dart into the woods, whispering leaves the only thing that remained of them.

There was a type of freedom that could be gained on the trails, even for a brief moment in time. Walking, trotting, or cantering with the group was relaxing and exciting all at once. I experienced so many firsts. My first trail ride. My first jump over a fallen log. The first time I galloped I felt like we were flying, the wind in our hair, and the trees whistling past us. I laughed at the exhilaration of it all even as part of me was scared I would fall. The other part of me was terrified that it would end too soon.

As a teenager I was daring. Daring in a way that I am grateful for because I took chances that my rational, adult mind would not allow. Perhaps it was the onset of hormones that made me less logical for a time and gave me the belief that I could do anything.

Challenges

All equestrians know that working with horses can be challenging. When I was learning to canter, we were taking turns in the ring. Line up nicely, and then one by one collect and transition from a halt to the canter. Easier said than done, of course. My horse began to buck. He kept bucking and bucking, full rodeo-style. Five bucks later I flew off, landing with a plop on the ground. I stood up, dusted myself off, and felt inordinately proud when my trainer called me Superman. This was the first time I ever flew at a buck and it would certainly not be the last. I can't recall fear really, and I don't recall being hurt at the time. It was my embarrassment, however, that remains vivid. What did I do wrong? Why did my horse react like that when none of the other horses bucked? I became wary to canter for a time because I didn't want to be embarrassed if I did something wrong.

I guess I finally got that cowgirl experience I'd always been wanting, just not in a way that I expected! But what do you do when you fall off a horse? You get back on and try again. Do not end the ride on a bad note.

When I felt confident about my riding, I could not be stopped.

4

HORSE SHOWS AND OH NO'S

*M*y confidence came along slowly. Confidence is a funny thing because it is slow to build and quick to deflate. I continued to lesson and move up session after session, always progressing. Everything in school came so easily to me, and I never had to study. The barn was the same way for me for many years.

I learned an extraordinary amount during those idyllic years, and it's funny how I can remember certain things so vividly, especially as they relate to supremely naughty horses. I learned the basics of steering and equitation, how to post on the correct diagonal, and how to correctly transition to the canter. That one had a few hiccups that resulted in bucking, but I learned! Always move forward.

In retrospect, there was a lot that I wish I had learned. Galloping in the woods was amazing, but I never learned how to tack a horse. The very basics of horsemanship I had to learn from books rather than personal experience and did not have the opportunity to practice. All equestrians should know these basic aspects of horse care.

I moved up through the riding levels and as a teenager I entered my first schooling show. Not a competitive person by nature, I was curious but not really sure what to expect. I ended up having a great time! While my memories are fuzzy, (this was a long time ago), I remember it being just like our lessons and I was quite comfortable.

As a result, I proudly won 2nd place in my first schooling show! Like most teenagers I felt like I couldn't fail. Here I was at my first ever horse show and winning that red ribbon right out of the gate. It certainly helped my confidence, but it also set me up for future disappointment because I thought all horse shows would be that easy.

On that exultation my trainer encouraged me to enter the next competitive show at the barn. Other barns would be competing, but I would be on my home turf with an advantage, or so I thought.

That day is seared into my memory. I had very little sleep because I'd been up all night nauseated with flutters of anticipation. I was at once excited and nervous considering the unknowns.

Morning dawned cold and rainy on that fateful day. I was unsure where to go, and my parents had no idea. We were all green newbies. The barn was lit up and drew us in, warm and inviting on that dreary day. My beautiful chestnut horse, whom I drew at random was groomed, tacked, and ready to go for me. I led my horse, the infamous Flame, to the mounting block. We were ready to head into the schooling ring to warm up, but my stomach was heavy with nerves.

It has never surprised me how empathetic horses are with their riders. I've seen it day after day and Flame was no exception. Headstrong on the best of days, he sensed my unease and decided the barn was infinitely more comfortable. The big chestnut gelding wheeled around and trotted forcefully back to the barn with me still astride and almost losing my head at the door. I confess that I let him do this. It was the "Gray Pony Incident" all over again. I felt out of control, unable to control my horse, and I completely shut down. This gelding knew that I wasn't ready, and I ceded control to him. Shaken and trembling, I let my horse decide for me and then I used it as an excuse not to ride. I dismounted, put him back in the stall, and scratched the show.

There was too much noise, too much chaos, and my horse was telling me that I wasn't ready. Or so I told myself as I walked away, my parents confused and trailing behind while arguing with me to stay.

STEPPING AWAY FROM IT ALL

$\mathcal{I}$ rode for a few months after my horse show debacle, but my anxiety became too great. My mother would drive me to the stables and my stomach would be in knots the entire way. Something that I loved was quickly becoming something that made me increasingly nervous, and I would find excuses not to ride.

$\mathcal{W}$ ith high school and the various homework and social activities involved, I made the decision to quit horse riding. I rode through to the end of the session. I'll never forget that last ride, which cemented it all for me.

. . .

On a gorgeous day we took a trail ride, one of my favorite things to do on horseback. I've never been much of a hiker but there is something about riding through the woods with your horse that has a truly grounding effect. You can leave all your worries behind and just enjoy being outside, in the fresh air, with an amazing animal. We are so lucky to spend our time with horses and I always appreciated that even on the tensest of days.

We returned to the ring after the trail and lined up to leave the ring in order. I was in the back when a car door slammed in the parking lot, causing my horse to spook and bolt. My heart was in my throat as we galloped directly toward the bottleneck of horses ahead. Instinct took over and I controlled my animal, with no injuries and no further spooking of any other horses. A blip in an otherwise calm day. I did exactly what I needed to do, but all I could think about were the consequences if I hadn't controlled my horse.

I dismounted, took care of my horse, and then left it all behind without looking back.

LIFE GOES ON

*L*ife goes on as it always does, and I faced my future without horses. I was relegated to the fact I would no longer experience the wind in my hair or the nuzzle of a soft, velvety nose because I would not have to deal with the gut-churning anxiety on the other side.

I spent a summer visiting colleges and universities. I had zero idea what I wanted to do with my life and was incredibly lost and confused. The two things I loved to do, I no longer felt confident enough to pursue. And in the mosaic of life not many children know what they want to be when they grow up and actually achieve the same. Regardless, I was accepted into several schools and even offered academic scholarships. Go me!

*I*t may seem like I'm indecisive when in reality I'm probably a little too decisive. I make decisions quickly, with instinct first and then sometimes logic. It was true both in quitting horse riding and the same went for choosing a school.

*M*y parents tried to entice me toward a less expensive school where I was given a scholarship. I still vividly remember my mother promising to lease me a horse if I went to one school in particular.

*T*alk about an amazing bribe!

*E*ven then after my break from horses, I was intrigued. What horse crazy girl wouldn't be? Ultimately, however, I knew that I would be so focused on my college experience that it would not be fair to a horse. There were too many debilitating unknowns.

. . .

here will I live?

Who will my friends be?

Will the courses be harder than high school?

What courses will I take?

What will I major in?

he questions kept coming and the idea of leasing a horse in addition to my college experience was too overwhelming. I respectfully declined and chose the university that spoke to my soul.

spent four years in college at the University of Delaware. It took only me choosing my first semester classes to determine my major in English with a minor in History. I wanted to work in publishing. Not as a writer though – that was a dream I'd left behind with the rest of those things I feared to fail at in life.

confess that I did write a lot in college, and not just for schoolwork. Stepping away and becoming independent meant trying new things. For a time, I was writing poetry and even attempted a few short stories. However, I would start these projects but never finish. It was not for lack of inspiration. I would stop because it would become too hard or I would decide to edit it again and again. My oldest and dearest friends were never invited to read my work because, in my mind, it was never good enough.

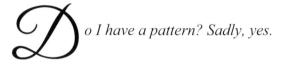 *o I have a pattern? Sadly, yes.*

I was able to distract myself with classes, parties, boyfriends, and time spent with friends. No regrets.

7

AN IRISH ESCAPE

I graduated college, and as a gift, my family planned a two-week trip to Ireland followed up by a few days in London. Ireland has always called to me with its lush landscape and rich history steeped in legend.

Ireland absolutely did not disappoint. Each town and village was more beautiful than the last, and I could feel my senses shifting, my imagination expanding past the confines I'd so skillfully placed upon myself those years ago. Breathing in the scent of the sea as the waves crashed on Inch Beach or walking the fields of Adare Manor in search of fairies in the wildflowers, I was free for a time from all the restrictions I'd placed on myself.

For the first time in years I took a deep breath and just enjoyed the moment. While it was a family vacation, I was an adult and chose to go off on my own for extended periods. I found myself buying a journal to document my thoughts and feelings, something I hadn't done in a long time. If you have never kept a travel diary, I highly recommend it. I recently pulled it out and began perusing it. Boy did it make me laugh! It was great to have insight into my 22-year old self and made me remember details that I had previously forgotten.

It seemed that Ireland was determined to inspire me in more ways than one. On our first night in Dublin, my younger sister and I stayed up until dawn with new Irish friends we'd made. In the invincibility of youth, we soaked up the new experiences and toured the city at night, which of course involved a horse-drawn carriage. I made friends with all the carriage horses and fell in love with one in particular who was determined to be my friend, giving me those breathy snuffles and nudges that I had missed so much in my years away from horses.

We drove south from Dublin and I remember vividly even after all this time, the most interesting bed & breakfast in Dundrum. The name eludes me but the rock garden adjoining the hotel was breathtaking. My travel diary brings me right back to the moment:

"I passed a chicken coop and a then a large, wild pasture. I was pleasantly surprised to find a sorrel

horse in the far, right side. I didn't call out or anything, but after a few minutes he walked up to me. He paused a few times as if unsure but let me pet his soft muzzle. I decided to name him Charlie."

There is a perfect example of how quickly I become attached to an animal. There were two dogs on the property that I noticed as we were leaving the bed & breakfast. Their fur was matted with burrs and thorns and they craved the attention my sister and I gave them. They clearly were working dogs or strays that were starved for human affection. I was the bleeding heart that wanted to steal them and bring them home with me after only a few minutes introduction. My parents insisted on leaving and my sister and I were driven away with tears in our eyes.

The very memory makes me happy and sad all at once. I remember the feeling and how those animals stood out to me after a chance encounter almost two decades ago. Some things make a lasting impression.

We continued on our journey, exploring the amazing vistas of Ireland. There were so many horses dotting the countryside, and I was incredibly inspired in so many ways. My parents wanted to golf when we arrived in Kerry, so I decided that I needed to go riding for the first time in about five years.

I was nervous to ride again. My stomach had butterflies

of anticipation and excitement, but I had no doubt whatsoever. I was doing this. I took a taxi to Rockland Stables in Killarney, and was very excited to meet my horse, Baggio. (If it weren't for the travel diary, his name would have been lost to the recesses of my mind). I informed my guide that I'd had previous experience and we set off on our 2-hour hack through the village, meadows, and woods with the barn dog in tow.

I doubt I can ever truly share the sense of euphoria that came with being back in the saddle. For the first time in a long while, I was happy to be riding and my muscles quickly remembered.

We walked our horses through the village, greeting neighbors and offering waves. We galloped across the meadows, our horses competing for the lead while the wind caught my laughter and carried it away toward the distant shore. I experienced the Ireland I knew was waiting for me through the entire trip. This moment was everything I wanted from my experience.

Two hours flew by and I could not have had a better way to spend my day. The barn owner had an appointment in town, so I was able to catch a lift and then walked the remaining three miles to our bed & breakfast. My jeans had chafed me from the stirrup leathers and by the time I arrived, I was both limping and exhausted.

For all the exaltation of my Irish riding experience, the next day packed a wallop. I woke in incredible pain, unable to move any muscle in my body. Even my eyelids hurt. My sister brought me ibuprofen and once that kicked in, I was able to get out of bed with her help and with the use of a blackthorn walking stick I had bought for my college boyfriend as a souvenir.

Note to self: if you haven't ridden a horse in five years it may not be the best decision to ride for two hours, full out. You will absolutely pay for it later.

8

ANIMALS IN THE CITY

*M*y amazing time in both Ireland and London was a breakthrough for me. It showed me that I needed both creativity and animals in my life to be happy.

I began work upon my return as an editorial assistant for *The Journal of Cell Biology* at The Rockefeller University Press in New York City. While it wasn't traditional publishing, I learned so much from working in scientific, technical, and medical publishing. My managing editor was opinionated, incredibly smart, and determined to make me into a better person.

I really enjoyed my work, but when I was off, I spent a lot of free time in Central Park, always seeking that oasis of nature that grounded me. Eventually I learned that the Central Park Zoo, part of the Wildlife Conservation Society, was looking for volunteers.

I vacillated for a year before the man I was dating, now my husband, encouraged me to go for the 6-week training course. What did I have to lose if I hated it?

You may imagine now that volunteering at the zoo fed my soul in a way that animals have always done for me. I'm highly educated and have a burning need to learn. Sharing what I know is only part of it. My passion for animals and my love of knowledge combined to create the perfect volunteer experience.

For four years I volunteered biweekly on Saturdays with some of the most amazing animal lovers and supporters that I've ever known. We worked in all kinds of weather no matter how bitterly cold, or intensely hot, and all for the love of animals. Accredited zoos and aquariums raise animals born in captivity, or rescue and rehabilitate those injured in the wild, to raise awareness. My volunteer coordinator said something that really struck a nerve, "People want to save what they love. So, teach them about the animals and show them how much you love them, so they will want to help them too."

And that's what I did. I brought a strong passion to my volunteer work at the zoo. I had a mission to help these animals. During summer when it was crowded, I enjoyed talking to everyone I could. During the cold winter months, I spent my time with the animals, photographing them, studying them, or simply being with them.

More than book knowledge, volunteering at the zoo gave me a sense of confidence and gratification.

My work world and my volunteer world were not hard to manage, and in fact, one helped the other.

After five years at The Rockefeller University Press, I moved to a job at John Wiley & Sons, Inc. Ever ambitious, I knew my ability to move up the ranks at the RUP was limited, despite the amazing educational opportunities, because it was a very small press. At Wiley, I had a lot of growth potential and was assigned to work on a troubled medical journal for my first account. Considering my ambition and drive to succeed, I devoted myself to this publication and made it prosper quickly and for the long term.

As my hard work became apparent to my bosses, I was given more responsibility. After a few years I applied for, and was given, a position to oversee both editorial and production for several titles. I now had the opportunity to manage employees around the world, a fantastic opportunity for which I'd worked incredibly hard and was very grateful.

The downside to this position, however, was public

speaking, of which I was terrified even though I was now overseeing board meetings and attending large conferences where I needed to be on display.

So, in the interest of moving forward I decided to face my fears. At the Central Park Zoo, penguin and sea lion feedings are done a few times a day for training and behavior enrichment. This gives the keepers the opportunity to interact with the animals, challenge the animals, and make looking for medical changes easy. At each feeding, a docent may be found describing what the zookeepers are doing, explaining why they are doing this, and imparting some information about the breeds.

Challenge accepted.

I began slowly by speaking at the penguin feedings during winter when it was quiet and the room was dark. As I found my confidence there, I pushed myself further by walking among the crowd while on microphone or inserting a few jokes. It was not long until I enjoyed giving the "Sea Lion Chat" during the summer to hundreds of eager visitors both in the zoo and walking through the park.

My passion for knowledge and for animals alike gave me the opportunity to work on something that terrified me. I made mistakes like anyone else, but instead of running from them as I did during my youth, I learned from them in order to become a better version of myself.

I succeeded because I pushed through my fears and used my passion as the fire that allowed me to keep moving forward.

PART II

CONFESSIONS OF A TIMID RIDER

9

MOTHERHOOD: THE TIPPING POINT

*C*onfession: **Motherhood changed my life.**

Being a mother changed me. When you are in your 20's everything revolves around you and the dreams you are making into reality. It's easy to live in a bubble of self-importance because you are living day to day and paycheck to paycheck. Heck, many of us at that age still don't know what our dreams are! I thought I had a dream. I realized even then that I'd veered off the path. Working in medical publishing was a far cry from writing fiction or being an editor at a major publishing house. But I was still working in publishing and making a career of it too. I was a self-starter, independent, and unafraid to ask questions. I was working my way up the corporate ladder and had ambition.

Then I got pregnant with my first child, Cameron. I

cannot describe the overwhelming love that I feel in my heart for my children. I always knew I wanted to have a career, but I was torn because I wanted to stay home as well. John Wiley & Sons, Inc. could not have been more accommodating to my situation. After submitting my resignation, my boss called me and convinced me to stay. The conditions: work from home but take a demotion. It was the ideal situation and one that many women would wish for. It worked extremely well until I had twins and they turned two years old. At that point, I had three children under the age of four and not a single one in school full time. I had to reprioritize.

From the first onset of pregnancy everything was about my child. It wasn't just hormones; it was reprioritizing my life. Suddenly nothing else seemed as important.

I chose to leave my career and focus on my family. It was the right thing for us, even if it was hardest on me. Forgive me for the gender stereotype here: it's different for men. While men are obviously integral to at least the start of reproduction, they are somewhat set apart. They watch while we deal with hormones, morning sickness, weight gain, and feeling like something else has taken control of your body.

Your body is no longer yours alone. Your whole life revolves around someone else.

The pattern tends to continue after childbirth. No matter

how modern or sensitive my husband is, (and he's a gem), the children were my primary responsibility and my first career.

Being at home without adult conversation or connections started to grate on my nerves after a while. I lost my sense of identity, my sense of self. Work had always given me a sense of pride. More, volunteering as a docent at the Central Park Zoo gave me a sense of satisfaction and time around animals.

In retrospect, I very likely had postpartum depression, especially after Cameron was born. I loved being home with my children and watching them grow up, being there for all the firsts, but I'd lost my sense of drive and creativity.

Unacceptable! But what could I do? I had only one option I could live with: find that person who I was always meant to be. Sounds easier said than done.

It all started with my weekly horse riding lesson.

Having three kids in two years was a bit of a surprise even though twins run in my family. I was able to work from home for a few years until it became apparent my young children needed more of my time. Lucky for me, I had a mother-in-law who wanted to help. I was able to take some time to myself once or twice a week to run errands, get my nails done, or OMG! do something for myself. After years of living in cities but dreaming of riding on horseback through the woods night after night, I made getting back into horseback riding a priority.

When my oldest daughter was eight months old, I decided to put on my big girl pants and make my dreams a reality.

10

OPENING THE BARN GATE

*C*onfession: I have more fear as an adult.

The decision to start riding again was not one I made lightly. I was out of the saddle for about 15 years, but I'd never lost my love of animals, horses in particular. Volunteering at the Central Park Zoo was a band aid, although an extremely welcome one. In the concrete jungle of New York City, it was an oasis that I found refuge in. But I still dreamed at night of riding through the woods or petting a velvet nose.

My husband is my rock. I honestly would not be where I am today without him. He has always supported me in anything I needed to do. He encouraged me to start riding again when I shyly expressed interest a few months after Cameron was born.

I'd been in a funk for months. Moving to Monmouth County, New Jersey, and not having any friends before I gave birth to Cameron was very isolating. I was depressed and overwhelmed. Jason pushed me to find something to hold onto for myself. My mother-in-law promised to take Cameron for me two days a week for a few hours so I could run errands. And I decided to use one of those babysitting days for horse riding lessons.

Monmouth County is the Gold Coast of New Jersey and ripe with green space, barns, and horses. The temptation could not be resisted! I found a local barn willing to teach a 31-year old woman with baby weight.

Victory Stables in Colts Neck became a source of comfort for me in that time. Warring between nerves and adrenaline, that single day of the week was the most I felt alive in years.

The hardest part was, of course, the first day. I arrived without knowing where I was going, whom my trainer was, or anything at all about the horse I would be riding. But when I arrived, that all slipped away. The smell of the hay, horses, and even manure evoked memories of happy times in my childhood. I immediately relaxed…until it was time to tack up and I had no idea what I was doing. Awkwardly, I asked for help and committed all I could to memory so I would remember what to do in future.

No one likes looking like they don't know what they are doing. Of course, I was wearing yoga pants, 15-year old rubber boots, and a velvet show helmet circa 1994.

My trainer, Walley, was incredibly patient and had a dry sense of humor, something I appreciate. We hit it off right away. Jupiter, the aging Thoroughbred dressage horse, was the perfect first mount back.

I thought to myself, "I've got this." Then I mounted quite awkwardly.

I don't know what I expected. It was shocking to realize that when I mounted up on to that old Thoroughbred that I was much further off the ground than I remembered. Fear kicked in, true fear; the fear that comes with realizing that I have small children at home who rely on me.

But this time, I didn't stop.

Jupiter was probably only between 15-16 hands, a small horse, and yet I felt incredibly high off the ground. Suddenly the mounting excitement turned to intense anxiety. The 'what ifs' began.

What if I fall?

What if I hurt myself?

What if I can't take care of my baby?

What if I'm being selfish?

The list went on and on. But I did not dismount or walk away despite my trepidation. I moved Jupiter forward into a walk while my trainer evaluated my seat and what I remembered from my childhood. It turns out I remembered a lot! My muscle memory kicked in and all those lessons must have drilled into the deepest, darkest recesses of my brain, because when I began to trot, I immediately got the correct diagonal. Success!

I felt awkward, (that word again), but I kept riding and was incredibly proud of myself when I completed that first lesson. Feeling this amazing animal moving underneath me, responding to my smallest aid, gave me a huge sense of exhilaration and confidence that I hadn't experienced in half a lifetime.

For more than an hour, I connected positively with a 1000 pound animal. I was HEATHER, not "mommy" or "wife." I felt alive in a way that I had been missing for a long time. I touched a part of my childhood that day and overcame my fears to pursue something that I needed.

I took baby steps to get comfortable again. My passion was reignited, and I fell in love with that horse like I've fallen in love with a number of other horses over the years. Each animal has something to teach me, and the ones that made me most nervous taught me most of all, even when I couldn't see it at the time.

Adulthood and all my experiences over the years has given me the most important lesson of all: the confidence to ask questions. I wanted to learn everything about horses. I learned how to groom and tack up a horse. I followed my trainer around and stayed late to watch other lessons. I watched groundwork exercises and took mental notes for when I would finally own my own horse. I became a thirty-something working student so I could learn the inner workings of a barn and did turn-out and feedings. I asked all the questions I was afraid or too shy to ask years ago. I've NEVER stopped asking questions.

That day changed the course of my life.

11

LIFE IS UNPREDICTABLE

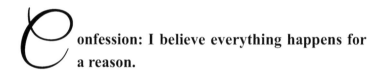

onfession: I believe everything happens for a reason.

That first day back in the saddle as an adult was life changing. I progressed, slowly but steadily, and Jupiter remained a favorite of mine. Change, albeit scary, was good for me, and I would periodically ride other horses.

One day I rode a beautiful mare named Lizzy. We were minding our own business, trotting along, when one of the stable hands threw a pile of wood down outside the outdoor ring, creating a sudden, loud cacophony. Lizzy bolted.

My first reaction? Surprisingly, it wasn't fear. It happened so fast my instincts kicked in. I simply went with her and when I was balanced again, shifted my weight and used my aids to slow her down.

My heart raced from adrenaline and fear. Horses are unpredictable, but life is unpredictable. Things are bound to happen, but I handled it well, if I say so myself. When I shut my brain off and just acted, I did exactly the right thing.

My trainer was incredibly proud and said, "Now I know that you've definitely ridden before!" It made me laugh because he was right. This was certainly not the first time I'd ridden a spooking horse, and it likely won't be the last. But nothing truly horrid happened. No falls, drags, or injuries occurred that day.

One of my favorite shows on television is Big Brother on CBS. There are so many reasons I enjoy it, but one is the utter voyeuristic aspect of people-watching at their most intimate. There is just something about creating stress in a closed environment with multiple personalities and seeing how they react; it's a modern day *Lord of the Flies*. The tagline for the show is, "Expect the Unexpected." This is an apt description for life with horses as well because no matter what, at the end of the day, horses are prey animals. They respond to stimuli and we cannot predict what the response will be.

It is this unpredictability that makes me a timid rider.

By nature, I'm not spontaneous. I'm a planner, an organizer, and somewhat type A. This has changed by necessity since motherhood, but I still find comfort in routine.

So why then the draw toward horses who are by very definition unpredictable? I really can't say. But I do know that they've made me a better person. Embracing the spontaneity of life, even in my own timid way, has opened doors. I've overcome my fears to start not one, but two equestrian businesses.

12

CREATING A NEW DREAM

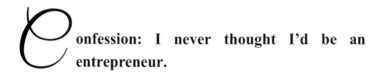

onfession: I never thought I'd be an entrepreneur.

There were many occupations I envisioned for myself during childhood. Horse breeder, veterinarian, author, publisher... but never a small business owner. Why? Maybe it was my lack of creativity or vision perhaps, or yet another visible sign of my lack of self-confidence? I'll let you decide.

As my children aged, soon came the much anticipated first day of Kindergarten for my young twins. While many mothers lament their youngest leaving the nest, I was anticipating a champagne brunch and perhaps even a movie all by myself. For seven years I had only small snippets of time to call my own and all within a limit to get back to the babysitter at the designated time.

Judge me if you want, but I am a better mother when I get to miss my children a bit.

The impending full school days left me with a huge question mark. What should I do now?

I was lucky to have a choice. My husband and I were financially stable, and I didn't have to work. While we dealt with meeting our budget like every other family, there was no looming requirement for me to return to work. But I didn't see the justification in staying home all day when my children were at school. This works for many, but I knew it wasn't enough for me. I wanted to feel smart again. Useful. Appreciated.

All women feel unappreciated from time to time, and I was no different.

I sent out feelers to my previous company, John Wiley & Sons, and was met with open arms. Most stay-at-home moms aren't so lucky after several years away. But I hesitated to take the offered position despite the amazing opportunity and generous salary offered. It meant long hours, a commute, and a lot of travel. It would mean a nanny for my children.

My husband, Jason, supported me. Whatever I decided, he would welcome because he wanted what was best for me and our family. After all, I'd been home for years while the girls were small. Now I had the unique opportunity to make a change.

Ultimately, I declined the offer because it didn't feel right.

My husband asked me this simple question, "What do you want to do?"

It was a huge question with no good answer. I had zero idea. A few months went by and my friend, and riding partner, mentioned being at the barn and watching an energy worker tending to a horse. She described the reaction in amazement, and I was intrigued. I never knew that equine massage therapy and energy work could be a career.

With my organized little mind, I had to do some research. I loved the idea of helping horses and making a career out of it. My husband was also intrigued but unwilling to support the idea without a thought-out business plan.

Two months later, I presented a 30-page business plan to my husband. He was a bit shocked because while he respected my dream, he never believed I would put so much effort into it. Never underestimate the determination and drive of a woman with passion.

I had passion in spades. I felt so strongly that I was doing the right thing for myself, but the thought of starting a business was terrifying. After all, I lived thirty-six years living one way. I stood on the precipice of something potentially big. I was taking all my education, experience, knowledge, and history and throwing it all away on something completely new and risky. After all, most small businesses don't succeed.

When I took time to think about it, I was terrified. I will confess this never would have been an option without my husband. We were financially stable, at least enough to try this for a few years. My husband gave me a three-year cap. The deal? He would invest half of the start-up fees, and if the business wasn't providing income in three years then I would find a part-time job to supplement my income, or lack thereof. It wasn't that he didn't believe in me. In fact, quite the opposite was true. My husband was impressed that I showed passion and motivation, something he hadn't seen from me in quite a long time.

My partner and I became small business owners of Bridle & Bone Wellness in June of 2016, to provide sports massage therapy to horses and dogs in our area. This was the beginning of an amazing ride but not without its learning curves, of course. I've always been a self-starter but never owned a business nor had a partnership. I've certainly made mistakes.

The positives absolutely outweighed the negatives. We

had a small but regular group of clients after only a few months of launching. In December of 2016, I began the blog, Bridle & Bone, to address common questions we had from clients. Writing, and sharing my writing, was infinitely more terrifying.

What I came to realize was this... I thought that I left my education and experience behind to turn a corner. But that wasn't true. Yes, I've started a new chapter that had a lot of pitfalls. But every single job I had in my life, my college classes, even motherhood set me on the course that I'm on today. I've used more of my knowledge and experience in this venture than I did on anything before.

Studying English literature helped me with creative writing, while my minor in Business and Technical Writing helped me with newsletters, brochures, educational writing, and even designing and building our website. More, my volunteer work at the Central Park Zoo helped me to use my passion in public speaking at vendor events and lunch and learns. Finally, my time as a working student at the barn helped me as a massage therapist because I knew how to read animal behavior.

Even with all this though, I'm still continuously learning.

13

ORIGINS OF AN EQUESTRIAN WRITER

*C*onfession: I never thought I'd be a writer.

I remember it clearly. The two-sided push from both my client and my business partner while chatting during a massage session on day last fall that created the origins of becoming an equestrian writer.

"You should write a blog!"

The idea had niggled at the back of my mind for a while. I've been writing, privately, since I was a young girl. Of all things that I loved as a child, it was horses and writing. But I held myself back. Very few people have ever read my writing. I was unwilling to take criticism, which I expected in truckloads. Eventually, I let self-doubt stop me from even trying anymore. I did not pursue my dreams because I feared failure.

What could I possibly write that others would read? What makes what I have to say so important?

The last few years has brought so many incredible changes both personally and professionally. I chose not to return to publishing and a regular salary. Instead, I chose to start my own business. A huge leap of faith and a gigantic risk. After all, we all know how often small businesses don't make it.

But starting my own company gave me the confidence I apparently needed. I'm an equine and canine sports massage therapist, and I'm incredibly proud of it. To have both my business partner and client say to me that they would be interested in my writing was really meaningful to me. It was the nudge that I needed.

But what to write? I don't own a horse yet. I love horses, but my confidence on them goes up and down depending on any given day. It's often a gradual increase in successes followed by something that makes me take a few steps back. Then I sat and thought about it. Why not write about this very thing? Surely other equestrians have felt like I do at some point?

I decided to write for myself and not worry anymore what others thought. Easier said than done, but I did it. I scribbled out my thoughts on a notepad because that was the nearest thing available. The words simply poured out of me like racehorses at the starting gate just waiting to be unleashed.

I surprised even myself with this visceral need.

I started with the intention to write primarily about "safe" topics I deal with everyday in my practice such as health and wellness for horses and dogs. But if holistic wellness is the brain of the blog, the heart of *Bridle & Bone* is my personal experiences as a returning adult equestrian. The "Confessions of a Timid Rider" series is my personal diary: a glimpse into my deepest thoughts, feelings, triumphs, and insecurities about riding.

"I wrote my first blog post in a busy kitchen while my children played, and my dogs begged for food."

I didn't start blogging as a way to gain readers or to earn money. I started blogging because I had something to say and I hoped it would help other people. Writing these posts are terrifying yet they give me solace. The very act of writing helps me to identify what I am doing that I can make better. Sharing my story? Less scary than I initially thought. The positive feedback was overwhelming, not only from equestrians, but from others who have faced their fears to do what they love.

One reader commented:

"Great post. I found your blog via Google, but it was

just what I needed today. I am in a full-blown funk this winter with an endless string of bad rides, strange "mistakes" that led to falls, and bizarre illnesses and injuries. Coming off of an awesome season last year with 100% plans to move up, I now find myself dangerously close to the spring season starting and zero confidence in my ability. Like you said, one option is to "step back," but I know that is not the answer. I have read and studied every sports psychology book on the planet and upped my riding to almost daily adding in every "trick" to improve…yet I find myself in constant, "how did that happen" lessons. I have decided it is a funk or a phase that we just have to get through…it might take lot of sweat and tears, (and maybe a little blood)…but I just have to gut through the funk and get back to the good."

Knowing that others not only related to my story but were inspired to power through and face their own fears, is a gift I never dreamed.

I am so proud of how much I have learned and thankful for the people I have met. Gone are the days where I sit nervously before hitting "Publish." Now I am proud to share my story. I've realized that there are a lot of equestrians who can relate to my journey. Seeing how far I've come in just a few months gives me the strength to keep pushing myself forward and try new things. I've been interviewed on camera and off;

interviewed authors and eventers; written guest posts and sponsored reviews; written for top equestrian magazines; and even written a book or two. My confidence rose at all of the success in less than two years of blogging.

Will I always be successful? No. But I hope to learn from my failures as much as from my successes.

For years I let the fear of not being good enough to write stop me from even trying. My blog provided me with a freedom that I never expected. More than anything, blogging has taught me to trust myself, my writing, and to take chances.

What do I mean by chances? Glad you asked, dear friend. I mean my ability to bare my innermost secrets to whomever will read them.

I now take the very things of which I was afraid and turn them into challenges to conquer.

Case in point: this very memoir. I've been writing almost my entire life. My need to put ideas and creativity to paper has always been inside me. But less than a handful of people had ever read my stories before publishing my blog. The fear of judgment, of being less than I was in another's estimation, was too much to bear at times until the need to share my story became more important.

This is the heart of my writing. I found that my personal stories were the ones with which my readership really identified and engaged. Whether you love horses or not is not the issue. My writing is about facing my fears and doing what I love despite those fears and overcoming the odds in my way whether they were self-imposed or imposed by others.

Show me the person who has never felt self-conscious? The person who never felt they were less because of the way others saw them?

The irony is that I always rebelled at being like everyone else. I was never afraid to stand up for myself or stand out from the crowd. I never cared what the masses thought, and I was never bullied because it didn't matter to me. I was confident in myself. I was confident with everything but my writing and now my horsemanship. That alone should signify the importance of these two things in my life.

Yet here I am now. I've never been prouder of myself because despite my fears of failure, of judgment, I am putting myself front and center. Bridle & Bone has received so many wonderful commendations from readers around the world. More, the comments I receive on the blog and in private communication tell me I'm doing something important. These gave me the confidence to publish my sassy little book, *Equestrian*

Handbook of Excuses, and attend the Equus Film Festival as an author. I did not expect my book to win an award, but I put myself out there and met some of the most amazing people. Many of the authors, publishers, filmmakers, and equestrians from around the world were in attendance.

These connections, many of them now friends, further tell me that I'm doing what I need to do with my life. As a result, I've learned so much about my voice, about publishing, and even secured work writing for several magazines.

The moral of my story? Sometimes the very thing you are most afraid to do is the very thing you have to do to be happy and successful.

14

CONFESSIONS OF A TIMID RIDER

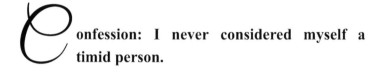

onfession: I never considered myself a timid person.

im·id

ˈtimid/

adjective

1 .showing a lack of courage or confidence; easily frightened.

.   .   .

I am not normally a timid person. Don't let my confessions fool you. If you met me on the street or at an event, "timid" is not something that would come to mind; quite the opposite, in fact. Even more, most people would classify me as an extrovert or having "high energy."

*T*hose who know me best know that while this isn't for show, I have limited ability to keep up that level of energy. While growing up, many children in my elementary school referred to me as a "snob" because I was quiet and tended to observe rather than participate. These were friends making these comments, not just random children. Frankly, I found it shocking but took it to heart to understand what I was presenting to the world. Truly, I was happiest reading a book or writing in my bedroom.

I made an effort to become more extroverted because I didn't like being labeled a snob, especially when it was the opposite of truthful. Coming into my own in junior high helped that a lot and I made pointed efforts to be more boisterous. Of course, sometimes I did this with a little too much energy. Now it's as natural as breathing…but only for limited times, as it is quite exhausting.

*I*s this a facade? I don't believe so – I simply adapted. Something wasn't working for me and I took measures to change. I still do things I don't want to do, because that's being an adult. I don't always have to like it. But I will admit, sometimes it is the best thing for me.

I refer to myself as timid in horsemanship.

I have a lot to learn. I don't mind admitting when something is beyond me or asking a question. I don't even mind falling. However, I fear the unknown. I fear that while I love horses, I'm only an okay rider. I fear that I will fail at something I love beyond all reason.

I can admit when I make a mistake. I take lessons for someone to point out those mistakes to me. And many times, I welcome them because I learn with lots of positive reinforcement thrown in for good measure.

I learn visually and that can't be found everywhere. I'm lucky that I found a trainer who understands me, and who gives me what I need to be my best.

*F*or example:

*T*rainer 1: "Don't pull on his mouth, create impulsion from behind."

Trainer 2: "Soften your hands, and follow his mouth. Now wiggle your leg. Good, feel how he moves better from underneath?"

*W*ords have power. I know that better than anyone else. Trainer 1's comments have a negative feel, and because I'm so sensitive to hurting another, they make me feel like I'm harming the horse, even when that is not the intention. Trainer 2 describes what to do in a way that I can understand and goes on to tell me when I'm following correctly.

· · ·

I don't consider myself very sensitive, but I guess that would be a lie. We, all of us, are sensitive about something.

*R*ecently, someone had advice about my riding. This person was concerned because someone told her I'd been having trouble and she offered her help. All well and good, right? Unfortunately, the person was watching me without my knowledge, with a limited view, and only a portion of my riding. That person did not see me move past that stiffness and really stretch, nor did this person see me practice and get better. More, they did not offer their help at the time; instead, they said something to someone else, making me feel terrible. One, I didn't agree with the assessment, but two, I felt like I was being spied on and judged. Why do I let that get to me?

I dried up my tears and got on my horse to prove to myself that it was false information. Everyone has a bad day, but I was so incredibly embarrassed. My trainer had never seen me do what I was accused of and felt that if the person couldn't say it directly to me, they should bring their concerns to her.

I was incredibly self-conscious for months after that, and it took me a long time to push through the nervousness I felt riding in front of other people again. Even now in mixed company I am just slightly more tense and unwilling to push myself or my horse for fear of looking stupid. But I am a work in progress.

I have a lot of amazing rides where I feel like a million dollars and my horse and I are communicating beautifully. So why do I focus on the one negative?

*H*uman nature, I suppose. I do dislike this about myself. I'm a work in progress. Aren't we all?

15

FOR THE LOVE OF A THOROUGHBRED

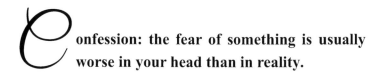

onfession: the fear of something is usually worse in your head than in reality.

Certain breeds have reputations, especially Thoroughbreds. Many people assume they are delicate, nervous, and spirited. Off-track Thoroughbreds that used to be racehorses? Forget it! So then why are they so popular with equestrians?

I confess I used to be on of "those" people. I said I would never want a Thoroughbred because I thought the breed would be too much for me to handle.

I bought in to the stereotype for a long time. Funnily enough, the schoolmaster I started back with at the age of 32 was a Thoroughbred. I thought to myself, "This is just a fluke." After all, Jupiter was a senior. As a "timid" rider I promised myself I would stick with the sensible Quarter Horse and stay in my comfort zone.

After several years of riding again as an adult, I became a working student. I worked on the ground with a lot of Thoroughbreds and other breeds doing turnout, feeding, etc. My favorite horse to spend time with while working came to our barn as a retired racehorse. Earthly Delights is Kentucky-bred and was retired from racing after he had surgery to remove a bone chip in his knee at three years old. He spent about six months in rehabilitation and then came to our barn to be restarted as a hunter/jumper.

For about two years I rode Delight regularly. I was very nervous in the beginning, but excited. After all, I knew this horse well on the ground., but I had a misconception of riding a young off-track Thoroughbred (OTTB). My trainer reminded me of that and assured me he is the same on the ground as he is under saddle. We have had our ups and downs, sure, but he is steady and patient, (mostly), even when I'm going through a funk.

Earthly Delights has so much personality. While he knows his own mind, he is forgiving and smart. His biggest foible is that he is totally grouchy while saddling, but once he's tacked up, he's a puppy dog. I love that I can ride him on the trails, jump him in the ring, and then watch him play with my daughters. He is very careful – he's just a grump. I'm in love with Delight and officially a convert to OTTBs. His owner told me that he likes me! This is the biggest compliment because he only likes two people. I thought it was unrequited love, but apparently I have a chance.

I was curious what other Thoroughbred owners and riders love most about their horses. I posted a request on the OTTB Connect Facebook group and asked for equestrians' favorite traits of this particular breed.

Here are some of my favorite responses:

"His eagerness to do anything I ask of him even if it's new and scary. He's a smart boy and would do anything I ask!"

"Smart and brave. Both have saved my bacon so many times. Quirkiness and attitude is a plus."

"Their heart. My Thoroughbreds never say no; they always try to do what I ask of them."

"Their heart, willingness to give 200%, quirky personalities, lmao! And, of course, their beauty and strength."

"Work ethic, strong connections, versatile."

"Their huge hearts! I love that they will keep trying and

trying. I also love their competitiveness and their stamina. It's fun that they love their work."

The responses were fast and furious, including some amazing photos. OTTBs and Thoroughbreds in general are often misjudged. One thing that really stands out to me is their heart. Many people most love Thoroughbreds because of their desire to form a connection with their humans, but let's not forget those quirky personalities!

I know that Earthly Delights is a sassy, funny boy who makes me laugh. Hard to forget too is that he's absolutely stunning to look at.

My trainer knows that I want to steal Delight away; now if I could only get my husband to finance it…

My 40th birthday came and went without my hoped for present. Wishful thinking, I suppose.

So, forget the reputation of OTTBs that you think you've heard. Give one a chance. Just like with any breed of animal, keep in mind some personalities need a more experienced "person." That being said, there is a reason Thoroughbreds and OTTBs are so popular, and it's not just for their athleticism. Thoroughbreds are smart, willing, versatile, and love bonding with their human.

Don't we all try to avoid stereotypes? They can be

insidious, and we don't even realize. I assumed a breed in particular was too much horse for me, and yet I was proven wrong time after time. In fact, this breed challenged me and taught me about myself as a rider, and as a person.

16

THINKING TOO MUCH

*C*onfession: **I think too much.**

I say that I am a timid rider, but the truth is I'm a *thinking* rider. I second guess myself. I have overcome a lot of insecurities, but my confidence level goes up and down like a roller coaster. Luckily, I have more ups than downs these days.

Looking back, I think of how much I've learned. I've taken baby steps, so I feel comfortable, but what's the rush? I don't compete in shows. I am not a professional. I ride for the love, the joy, and the passion of horses. Every day I spend with them on the ground and mounted is a blessing for which I will always feel grateful.

I don't think I can change the fact that I think too much.

My husband says the same thing about me at home. I am a very cerebral person. I read constantly; I learn voraciously. So, of course, I will take my lessons and "think" about what is working and what is not.

The problem is when I think too negatively and have trouble moving on from that. For example, a few months ago I had a scary incident. Delight and I were coming into a jump too slowly. He lost his balance, tripped over the rail, and we both started to fall forward.

This moment was one I dreaded since I became a mother. The thought of falling off and hurting myself in front of my children was something that plagued my nightmares and caused severe anxiety.

In slow motion, I can still see Delight's nose touch the ground. I slipped slowly down his neck, clinging for dear life. All I thought in that moment was if I topple over his head, he might become more unbalanced and land on me. So, I ever so slowly picked myself up and scooted back, lifting Delight's large Thoroughbred head up to help him regain his balance.

We were okay. That time. But I was shaken. I did not fall. Delight did not fall. We regained our balance, no one was hurt, and nothing bad happened. But I kept replaying the scene in my mind…the WHAT IF factor. The image became stuck in my head for the rest of our lesson, and I could not let it go.

"Get over it," my trainer called out.

It was obvious I was upset because I was shaking. Thank goodness Delight is hard to ruffle. So much for a crazy OTTB, right? I trusted him, but I didn't trust myself enough. My trainer made me catch my breath and before I could dwell, I had to do it again.

It wasn't pretty, but I did it again.

It was one scary incident, where I didn't even fall, and no one got hurt. But it resulted in MONTHS of me overthinking and being nervous to jump him again. My trainer did what I needed to rebuild my confidence; we went back to groundwork, transitions, and ground poles. Basically, I wanted to do anything but jumping.

Finally, after a few months we had a "breakthrough," in my trainer's words. It meant so much! She has been so patient, and we worked so hard that when it came time to jump again, I didn't even hesitate.

And we were perfect! Beautiful pace, extended trot in, canter out on the correct lead.

We had to laugh because after that amazing compliment she could see the gears turning in my head, revisiting what I did well and what I could work on.

I'm a perfectionist, so I am highly competitive with myself. I don't need to place higher in the ribbons than others. I need to know that I didn't make any mistakes. I am unfair to myself. I have incredibly high standards because I know what I am capable of, and I'm not sure that I've reached my goals yet. What I need to do is get out of my own way.

I am so grateful to learn with horses. We have a lot to teach each other and I'm still trying to convince my husband that buying Delight is the right move for me, even if he isn't the right horse for my daughters.

17

STRUGGLING WITH CONFIDENCE

*C*onfession: **I struggle with confidence.**

Timidity grew after coming back to riding as an adult and having children. I think it is not so much about being timid, but not always having enough confidence in my own riding ability or my post-baby weight. Confidence comes and goes like waves on the sand.

That almost-fall scared me and my children just so happened to be at the barn. I was so concerned with them seeing me get hurt that I panicked and got upset, but I did finish my ride. As nervous as I was to put my insecurities out there, I got some amazing feedback from other riders and readers when they saw my story. Others have gone through similar situations, whether as a rider, writer, or something else entirely.

Thankfully the very act of writing helped me to turn a corner, and I've taken baby steps to get my confidence back. I can honestly say that I am in an amazing place now.

Funny how things shift so quickly. It takes one "scary" ride to shake my confidence and months to get it back. We all have our different versions of what a bad ride can be, whether it is spooking and perceived misbehavior by our horses, a bad fall, or not meeting our own expectations. Frustration with ourselves can be enough to set us back.

I often fall into the latter category. I am very hard on myself and am very in my head during a lesson with my trainer. Are my knees gripping? Open my hips. Are my shoulders back enough? Sit up. Do I have enough contact with my reins? Why aren't I getting the correct lead? The list goes on. Sometimes I want to tell myself to, "Be quiet and ride."

So, what did I do to get my confidence back? I confess I'm always a work in progress. But here are some baby steps that I took that helped me. I hope they help you too.

Keep Riding

Don't let yourself stop doing what you love. Power through but change it up. If you're timid about jumping, then go back to transitions or work with ground poles.

If your horse has become spooky, work on desensitizing him/her to new situations from the ground then under saddle before you go on the trails. If you are fine at home, but crack under the pressure at horse shows, go to watch for a while as a bystander, act as groom, or better yet, attend schooling shows for practice. Take some of the pressure away. My trainer has changed up our usual lessons to play fun transition games, like "Command." It was a blast and impossible to be in your head when you have to go from canter to halt to sit trot whenever your trainer calls it out. So fun!

Groundwork

I think groundwork is often under appreciated. It builds respect between you and your horse and teaches you to safely interact in a controlled environment. If you cannot trust your horse on the ground and build a relationship of respect, how can you trust them under saddle? In addition to groundwork, spend time with your horse outside of riding. Play games, go for a hand walk, or just have quiet time together. Riding is only a small part of horsemanship.

Talk to your Trainer

My trainer is my therapist. Usually when I go to the barn, I release my anxiety and stresses of the day just by the familiar smells, nickers, and being outside; it grounds me. When I get in my head about my riding, my trainer is the one I tell. She is the person who pushes me to be better or talks me down. My advice is to open the lines of communication and explain what is going through your head, and then work through it together. After all, life is really a team sport.

Plan your Rides

When I don't have a lesson or trail ride, I don't usually have a plan for what I want to work on. I'm changing that. If I've had a rough time getting my horse to canter outside in the spring-like weather, that's what we work on. We go to the outdoor ring with all the horses playing in the paddocks and we work on transitions where he has to pay attention to me, or we keep going. I repeat the thing that gave me trouble in the first place, so we work through it until it doesn't become a big deal anymore.

Delight is high-withered and has a very bouncy trot. When I first started riding him it was so much work until I became used to him. Gradually I worked with him on collecting and sitting the trot, but it took a lot to get there. My trainer said that we've come a long way and are looking great. That means the world!

Exercise

My biggest problem with my equitation or riding skill

is that I am out of shape. I am a proud mother of three, but I have not exercised consistently in almost a decade. I don't ride effectively when I'm out of breath too quickly or am not strong in my core. Well, I'm proud to announce I have decided to jump out of that rut. It's still new but I've started exercising. I know! I'm still shocked. So far it's going great...I just need to keep at it. I'm not doing it to lose weight, (hopefully that will be a side benefit), but to make me a better, more efficient rider.

Alright folks, there it is my five-step plan to regain your confidence as a rider. I admit I have the benefit of writing my thoughts out and letting the world read them.

Eek!

But it does really help. With the change of seasons comes the opportunity to make changes for yourselves as well. I wish you all the best of luck. The chances are you are much better than you give yourself credit for. So, go easy on yourself. After all, we're only human.

18

TODAY COULD HAVE BEEN WORSE

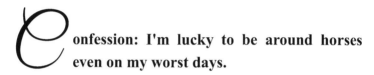

Some days just start all wrong. You know those days where you wake up late, you are out of cereal, or something happens to just put you in a MOOD?

I work a lot of weekends and Mondays tend to be my "day off," aka barn days. Monday is like my Saturday in a lot of ways and thus doesn't inspire the hatred that most 9-5ers have. I do carry over exhaustion from working weekends. Not an excuse, just a contributing factor.

Frustration

I am a pretty even-tempered person, very logical. I'm

also a Libra, and if it's to be believed, I tend to try and see both sides of an argument. Being an introvert does not help, as I don't like confrontation and tend to keep my feelings inside. These feelings build up and keep building up, until finally they explode. Usually the explosion is over something completely innocuous and unrelated.

But on occasion I carry some serious mad with me to the barn.

I Couldn't Find My Horse

I love, love, love my barn at Lancaster Equestrian Stables. There are three barns up for lessons and boarders and acres of lush paddocks for the horses to enjoy during turn out.

There was a rumor that Delight was going to be moved from his stall up top to rough board below, but I was not sure if or when it was going to happen. I did not see him in his regular stall and the name plate had been changed. I didn't see him in ANY of the stalls. I peeked over into the paddocks and called my trainer. She had asked for him to be kept in, so we assumed that he was moved below to the owner's barn and pasture. As a result, I packed up all my tack and went below.

Walking out to the paddocks I counted all the horses but

found no handsome bay in sight. I packed up all my stuff, again, and went back up top.

By then my trainer had arrived and we went searching in the paddocks together. He was indeed at the very end of the field, happily laying in the grass with no cares in the world.

By this point I was really not in the mood for a lesson. You know those days when you want to be there, but you don't really want to do the work? So over it.

My Horse is Testing Me, Life is Testing Me

After all his laziness in the paddock, Delight basically fell asleep on me in the ring too. I would ask him for the trot, and he would stop instead. When I refused to give in to him, he would toss his head and swish his tail in impatience. I'm telling you, this gelding was just not in the mood to work either. I didn't back down, but I knew that it was largely my fault. I was so distracted I was giving my horse mixed signals.

You know how horses are, testing you to see what they can get away with.

Some days the barn is a source of frustration, and on others it can be a source of comfort.

There are many reasons that I love the barn. I am lucky

that the barn where I ride is almost 500 acres of glorious hills and valleys that are reminiscent of a much less suburban area. It's truly an oasis in the heart of Monmouth County, New Jersey.

When I fight with my husband, get worried about my kids, or generally need a break from life, that's where I go. I head there sometimes with my camera but often just to sit and look over the horses grazing in the valley below... or like today, sobbing into the neck of my favorite horse because of a bad day.

Delight is generally the cranky sort and the perverse part of me loves it because his regard has to be earned. I respect that. Today rather than pin his ears at me, he came over the stall door and let me sob into his neck. He even hugged me a bit, which of course made me cry harder, but I felt better. Afterward, I sat on the tack box and just watched him and the other horses. Maybe I talked to him a little too. Sometimes the only therapist you need is someone who will listen and just be there for you.

The compassion and empathy of horses make for ideal listeners. Plus, they don't tattle on you.

I can't explain it. That feeling of walking into a quiet barn and hearing all the horses nicker to greet you. When it's just you and the horses munching in their stalls or grazing contentedly in their paddocks. The smell of horse and, yes, even manure is familiar and makes you feel safe. It's grounding, calming, and it is where I find my peace.

Somehow things don't seem quite so bad anymore. Today was a good day after all.

19

WHO NEEDS A HORSE HUSBAND?

*C*onfession: **My husband doesn't love the same things I do.**

*M*y husband is not a horse person. I cannot stress this enough. In fact, he's the opposite. He went from apathetic about the subject of horses to now dreading it all together. I definitely pushed him to this point with my obsession. I talk about horses constantly. I have a talent that allows me to turn ANY conversation to horses. It helps that I have a forum on my blog and social media to share my thoughts. Thank you to my followers and all those people who don't mind me talking about horses and dogs all the time! It may have saved my marriage.

. . .

I do want to clarify that Jason is completely supportive of my career and my passion. He's come to see me train once or twice. He works long hours and I ride during the week, so it's not surprising that he doesn't make it to the barn more often. The few horse shows I've competed in, he attends with the kids and takes pictures. Once he took a lesson with my trainer, (after years of pleading on my part). I mean, what's scary about getting on a 1200 pound animal that balks at loud noises?

*M*y husband had fun during his lesson and was a good sport about the whole thing. I was insanely excited and thought he looked so cute, even cuter because I knew he was just doing it to make me happy. While he had fun, it is definitely not his passion. His preferred sports are snowboarding and surfing, which is almost as sexy as riding horses.

*D*o I sometimes wish that we could take trail rides together? Yes, absolutely I do. He wants to go hiking or mountain biking, and I don't see the fun in it if I'm not on horseback. I see other couples enjoying their time together at the barn and think it would be nice to have that bond. Ideally, we would go on equestrian vacations and gallop the beaches in Ireland or round up cattle out west. But then reality intrudes.

The truth of the matter is that while my husband and I love each other, we are nothing alike. He's the yang to my yin. What I love most about Jason most is that he is just as independent as I am. I enjoy my hours at the barn and attend horse shows for fun; he goes snowboarding with friends or surfing in the nearby Atlantic Ocean. It's a pretty good system and it works for us.

We spend quality time together doing things we both like but have separate hobbies that we get to have for our own. The barn is my time, that every so often I share with my husband. Recently Jason took the day off work to celebrate our anniversary. The plan? Come to the barn for an hour and then lunch, a rare and special occurrence.

It would be nice to spend time together enjoying something I love, but that's just it, he doesn't love it. We have other things that we do together. I'd rather be at the barn with fellow enthusiasts who also think it is funny when a pony sneezes into my sandwich or spooks at a butterfly. After all, if I were to force my husband to ride a horse regularly, he might make me go surfing. Doesn't he know there are sharks in the ocean?

20

ALL CHILDREN SHOULD RIDE HORSES

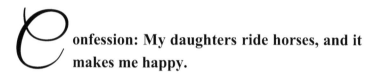

onfession: My daughters ride horses, and it makes me happy.

I'm an honest parent, or at the very least, I try to be. Perhaps I can be too honest at times. So, I'll be honest with you, my friend, that I'm not a helicopter mom. I'm the old school, "Go play and use your imagination, call me if you're bleeding," type of mom. Don't get me wrong. I love my children. They are hilariously funny, smart, and keep me on my toes. I'm just of the opinion that sometimes learning who you are and who you will become happens when you are given a chance. Keep yourself busy, make your own decisions, and make mistakes. That is why every child should ride horses.

My favorite time together is taking my daughters with me to the barn. Yes, it can be stressful some days. But the good outweigh the bad, just like motherhood in general.

When I used to do turnout and feeding, my little ones would help me sweep the aisles, hay the horses, or even clean tack, (their choice)! They girls would have plenty of time to play with the ponies or run around an empty ring pretending to jump fences as ponies themselves. But they have a strong work ethic and needed little incentive to contribute to barn chores. Often it was their own idea.

Just the other day my daughters asked me if they could stay late after a riding lesson to help their friend with barn chores.

When do spontaneous chores ever happen at home?

My oldest daughter has been riding horses since she was four years old at a local therapeutic riding center. She is tough, confident, and fearless. Basically she is everything that I am not as a rider. I cannot say that she wasn't any of those things before she started riding, but it has helped to shape her into a well-rounded child that I hope will maintain that confidence and sense of self through her teen years.

After all, how intimidated will she be by mean girls when she is used to being assertive with a 1000 lb animal who is feeling stubborn? She tells me that she wants to be a jumper, which is terrifying to me. She challenges herself every day and you know what? She'll rock at it because she refuses not to be awesome. She is my role model for life.

In May 2016, my 6-year old twins started taking riding lessons. For those of you who think that I pushed my hobby on them, please stop right there.

The twins had begged me for three years to take riding lessons, and I put them off. I would distract them and say, "Let's try dance," "Let's try gymnastics," or "Let's try soccer." As much as I love horses, it is an expensive hobby and I knew they would gravitate to it one day.

Who can put a price on passion?

I wish I started riding when I was 6-years old. It may not have changed my anxiety to be the best possible rider I can be, but all the things I'm learning now as an adult would have been that much better when I was young. A strong foundation makes for a strong person. It took me a long time to build a solid foundation of my own based on my passions.

Riding Horses Teaches Children Important Life Lessons

Exercise

This should be a no-brainer. For those of you who think

the horse does all the work, I suggest you mount up. Then call me in two days and tell me you aren't sore everywhere. I dare you.

Horse riding takes muscle, primarily your core and your legs, a quiet seat, quiet hands, and an effective leg mean muscle control and strength. Riding builds muscle and, further, it provides a cardio workout. Anyone who has ever collected their canter while doing circles has gotten a little winded. I can tell what shape I'm in by how many loops around the ring I can do without stopping to catch my breathe. Hint: it's not a lot. I applaud the endurance riders out there.

Get Outside

Do you ever stare at your child on their phone, tablet, or watching television and see a zombie? Growing up as I did in the 70's and 80's, I would spend the entire day outside and only come home after dark. That is different today with technology. Riding horses is an amazing way to get outside and spend time experiencing nature and get some fresh air!

Teamwork

You have to rely on each other. Horses will test you. They will get away with whatever they can, so you have to be confident and quiet. You can't be loud, obnoxious, and throw a temper tantrum when things are not going your way. Ask nicely, consistently, but firmly. You learn to work together.

Patience

Have patience with your horse, but most of all, patience with yourself. I struggle with this constantly.

Give yourself the room to make mistakes, understand what you are doing that isn't working, and make it better. My trainer never lets me end a lesson until we do something well. Always end on a good note. You know what? Each time I get just a little bit better. There is nothing more satisfying than a job well done.

Practice

Equestrians never stop learning. The best riders in the world have trainers. Every horse has something to teach us. Every ride is different, and every horse is different. What we bring to the barn from our personal lives affects how we ride. The more practice my daughters have, the better riders they become. And they learn that hard work is necessary for success. In order to succeed, you need to work hard.

How to Fall

It's a fact of horseback riding that falling is inevitable. I do not look forward to their first falls. I'm cringing even thinking about it as I have a house full of drama queens. (As I write this my six year old is hysterical because she scraped her knee on the driveway. For 20 minutes she has been sobbing, screaming, and scooting across the floor because she doesn't want to put weight on it. There isn't even blood. You would think she'd broken a vital appendage).

I've fallen many times over the years. Some falls were unavoidable, and others were because I wasn't balanced. The important thing is knowing how to fall safely and how to get back up again.

My funniest fall is when my girth loosened during a horse show as I was transitioning down from the canter. I called, "Hold up," and started slipping. I moved my horse out of the way and proceeded to slide steadily butt first onto the ground. Thankfully it was a schooling show. The judge actually gave me points for a graceful landing and because I stood up and bowed afterward. Sometimes you just have to laugh at yourself!

I realized I made a mistake by not checking my girth myself. But mistakes happen in life. It's not how you fall down; it's how you get back up again that can make all the difference.

How to Get Back Up Again

There is a well-known saying, "Get back on the horse." Falls can be scary. Your adrenaline kicks in and all you think is protect your head and get away from the hooves. But, scarier than the fall itself is the prospect of getting back on because you do not want to fall again. You have to get back on and try again because if you let the fear build up in your head, then you psych yourself out.

My children need to learn that just because you fall doesn't mean you can quit. Sometimes things happen that we don't like or we don't expect, but we have to keep going.

Compassion

Compassion is something that is extremely important to me. I want to raise my children to think of others and not focus so much on their own wants and needs. Narcissism is rampant in the world today. Riding horses is such a beautiful way for a barn rat to learn compassion. Equestrians learn very early that you must groom, tack, pick up manure, [ride], untack, brush down, and thank your horse. Riding is just a small part of horsemanship, although it's the one most people focus on.

Years ago, I was on a trail ride with my business partner and my trainer. We took our horses through the field and up into the woods. Almost as soon as we entered the woods the horse I was riding, Chico, started to rear a little. We were in the back and I called to my trainer.

Something just wasn't right. We turned around and I took up the rear again.

By this time the horses were all behaving abnormally. When my trainer got to the edge of the field her horse bolted. Robin jumped off, grabbed the reins, and called for us all to dismount. Danelle jumped off and her horse, Beach Boy, took off. Chico stayed with me until I jumped off. The second I left his back he bolted. The force of it pushed me off balance and I landed on my back hard. It was an awkward fall, but I protected my head.

I stood up, dusted myself off, and went to find my horse. There was no time for coddling myself. Heart racing, I felt something painful and looked down to see that I was covered in adolescent yellow jackets. I bolted out of the woods and across the field in blind panic.

You can imagine how comical it was for my trainer to follow me running across the field and hitting me with a riding crop to remove the wasps.

I was stung seven times, shaking with pumping adrenaline and fearful of an allergic reaction. Never in my life had I been stung before and I didn't know how I would react, especially to that many stings. I did not immediately seek medical help. Instead, we went and tracked down our scared horses. The entire time my horse was warning us and getting stung himself; yet they waited until we were safely dismounted before running away.

We hand-walked them all the way back to the barn. Then we washed them down, removed the stingers, and treated their wounds. I didn't have medical help until at least an hour and a half later.

The moral of the story is that equestrians take care of their horses first, always.

I will admit that getting back on another horse a few days later was scary. Our horses were not in the position to be remounted either physically or emotionally after their wasp interaction for several days afterward.

Focus on the moment.

When I care about something, I want to succeed and I work hard to be better. I am hard on myself because I know what I am capable of in life. When I don't perform to my expectations, I lose confidence in myself and bathe in disappointment.

Overall, riding horses has given me confidence I didn't have before. I have my down moments, sure; however, I know that I can handle situations that used to make me run in the other direction. Working with a young horse is a challenge that is making me a better rider, and I welcome it.

My children have the opportunity to work alongside these amazing animals. Horses have a lot to teach us about ourselves. To earn their trust and respect is something special.

Fun!

Horses are a lot of fun on the ground too! What is more fun than riding a horse? Pretending to be one yourself.

Let's not forget that riding horses is a whole lot of fun. My youngest was nervous to ride in her first lesson, but even though she was a bit tense, she had a huge grin on her face the entire time. The second she dismounted she asked when her next lesson was. It's hard to put into words the feeling riding a horse gives you.

Everyone should experience it at least once. It's not for everyone, but there is nothing else like it in the world. I'm so glad that my daughters can experience the same feeling I do.

Teaching Moments

Riding horses has taught me so many things. It's taught me patience, humility, strength, empathy, and determination. Most of all, riding horses has taught me to fight for what makes me happy. My passion does not always end in a great day and still causes me anxiety from time to time. But the good outweighs the bad. When I get on a horse everything else is less important for a time. My head clears and my endorphins kick in. Where even two years ago I would panic at being bucked, I now laugh and try to understand what I did to cause that reaction while keeping my horse moving forward. I may not have the best technique, but I've come a long way, despite my moments of self-doubt.

I want my children to get their hands dirty and not be afraid to assert themselves with confidence. I am proud that my daughters share my passion for animals. Who knows how long they will ride? What matters is that they fought for a chance to ride horses, they worked hard to earn their lessons, and they are having fun. Will they decide to follow a different path? If they do it will be their decision. The lessons they are learning now will be what makes them amazing adults that I will respect. We can all learn a lot from watching children open themselves up to new experiences.

After all, I want my children to know that if they want to be successful human beings, they need to do at least three things: ask politely, work together, and keep moving forward.

21

MY DAUGHTER IS MY HERO

*C*onfession: **My daughter is my hero, equestrian and otherwise.**

My daughter Cameron is special, as all children are in their own way. She is sassy, confident, intelligent, and did I say confident? She also has cerebral palsy. We don't know when she had a stroke, but she was diagnosed at 18 months old. Despite this though, she hit every developmental milestone and can do anything. The only difference is she has to work harder than others.

For those of you who don't know what cerebral palsy is, I'd love to tell you. Better you, I'll let the Cerebral Palsy Alliance tell you:

"Cerebral palsy is an umbrella term that refers to a

group of disorders affecting a person's ability to move. It is due to damage to the developing brain either during pregnancy or shortly after birth. Cerebral palsy affects people in different ways and can affect body movement, muscle control, muscle coordination, muscle tone, reflex, posture, and balance. Although cerebral palsy is a permanent life-long condition, some of these signs of cerebral palsy can improve or worsen over time."

There are many pediatric strokes survivors in the world, although it is a little talked of topic.

We are the proud parents of a stroke survivor.

Cameron has never known any different. While she may get frustrated at times, especially as she gets older, she is a fighter and good luck to the person who tries to tell her what to do.

Therapeutic Horse Riding

When Cameron was four years old she was recommended by early intervention to a local therapeutic horse riding center. Special People United to Ride (SPUR) has been a source of comfort, confidence, and excitement for Cameron these last four years. Best of all it is two miles from our home. We are extremely lucky.

I first brought Cameron to the barn when she was 18 months old. She fed the horses carrots and squealed with excitement. As an equestrian, who was I to deny the benefits of therapeutic riding?

I spoke with her trainer about our goals when she started. I wanted her to have the occupational therapy and physical therapy benefits of therapeutic riding. But also important to me as an equestrian is her learning to ride and handle a horse independently.

But my daughter has excelled with other life lessons also. First, to ask nicely but firmly. When working with horses you cannot be shy; don't give up and don't give in. Second, go with the flow. It's not easy to attend a horse show with a horse you haven't ridden in a year because your regular pony is sick. But as Cameron learned, you have to keep moving forward and be okay when life becomes unexpected. Third, be a good sport. My daughter is gracious to the other riders, kind to her horse, and no matter the ribbon she receives she leaves with a smile on her face. Last but not least, my daughter has learned the utmost confidence in herself. Anyone who meets my daughter says, "I would never know she had a stroke." We worked really hard to accomplish that. This is a true testament to her personality as she simply shines.

My Daughter is My Hero

I am a timid rider. Sure, I've come leaps and bounds over the years, but my kid blows me away. She has zero fear, which is terrifying to me as a parent. Apparently while she likes horse shows with flat classes, she prefers to jump. I am informed that not only does she want to be a pop star, teacher and mother, but also a Grand Prix jumper. She makes a conscious decision to challenge herself and take the more difficult path which is something that I have difficulty with in my own life. What parent wouldn't be proud of that?

Like me, Cameron feels strongly for her animal friends. She has a favorite horse, Woody, that she is madly in love with. I can't blame her; he is amazing.

I've often joked that Cameron would never leave her friends and the horses at SPUR, and she agrees. As she has gained skill and confidence, but she count certainly ride at my barn and take "typical" lessons. But my friends who run SPUR say I am not allowed to take her away from them. As if she would let me. She is loyal and true. I am so grateful to our friends in the PATH-certified* program for all they have given us.

There are a lot of things I can learn from my daughter. While she has challenges other kids don't have, she is open, honest, and kind. My daughter is someone that I respect and admire. She is my hero, equestrian and otherwise.

*PATH INTERNATIONAL. Professional Association of Therapeutic Horsemanship International (PATH Intl.), *a federally registered 501(c3) nonprofit, was formed in 1969 as the North American Riding for the Handicapped Association to promote equine-assisted activities and therapies (EAAT) for individuals with special needs.*

22

HORSE SHOW MOM

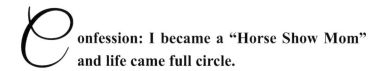onfession: I became a "Horse Show Mom" and life came full circle.

My youngest daughters had their first horse show. They had been riding horses for a few months and were so excited to have their first schooling show at the barn. I confess I was a little nervous for them. After all, I get terrible show nerves.

I've technically been a horse show mom a few times with my oldest daughter. She is strong, courageous, and cool as a cucumber. The twins are another story. They are much more high maintenance and one of them struggles with some anxiety, just like me. I was very nervous for this show because I didn't know how they would behave or react. My nerves went into overdrive, and I wasn't even the one riding!

The Day Before the Horse Show

Flash back 24 hours before the show. Anyone who has a significant other knows that they can be extremely frustrating. I had to work Saturday and asked my husband to have my daughter try on her older sister's show breeches. I needed to know if they fit; otherwise, I had to stop at the tack store on my way home from work.

Did this happen? No, it did not happen. My husband carried on with his day, continuously walking around the center island with the breeches in question folded nicely on the counter in direct line of sight. I will acknowledge that she wasn't feeling too well, perhaps nerves or fighting an infection, but no clothes were tried on that day.

I came home from work and went about my business as usual. At 7PM she was miraculously cured and wanted to attend the horse show the next morning. Of course, her older sister's show breeches were way too big.

I ran around like a crazy woman before the stores closed attempting to find tan pants that I could substitute for breeches, a button down shirt, and show ribbons. Because these have all apparently gone missing. Super. I was incredibly annoyed. It would have been a lot easier to stop at the tack shop after work and get all items instead of running to four different stores to find items that may be a good alternative.

The Horse Show

Getting the twins ready for the show was a little stressful. On any given day getting my children ready for school, much less of an event, is an exercise in patience. Luckily, they were both excited and Zoe didn't mind wearing tan khakis instead of breeches even if her clothes were a size too large, but she was a good sport.

It's a schooling show after all, which is a quiet show at our home barn for practice among friends. Walking in, I knew the judge and knew that she wouldn't be too strict about the show clothing for the littles. It was a huge relief.

All nerves aside, I was so proud of my girls. They had only been riding a few, short months. Nor had they ever ridden in that particular ring, in front of children and their parents, much less a judge. But the girls seemed absolutely unflappable.

I proudly led one of my daughters on her pony for the show.

Out of four lead line competitors, my two were the youngest and had ridden for the least amount of time. I had no grand expectations, only that they would have fun. And they did! The judge asked to speak to all the riders in the class and commented on what lovely posting trots they had.

We all came out winners that day, not because they received ribbons for attending, but because they tried their best and had fun. I proudly led my daughter in her first horse show; they had fun, and they loved every minute! My barn's schooling shows are such a lovely way for the girls to get their feet wet. It was a non-competitive horse show with our barn family cheering them on. I can't think of a better way to grow up and learn about life.

I hope my daughters learn from my successes and failures, but in the end, they need to make their own choices and live with them. Just like I did.

I'm a proud horse show mom.

23

STRUGGLING WITH MOTIVATION

*C*onfession: some days I'm not motivated to ride.

*H*orses are my passion, but I tend to doubt my skill and often question myself. I don't think I'm alone in that. Today I did not set myself up for success. In fact, I really made some poor decisions and struggled with motivation.

*E*xhaustion

. . .

When my barn has pony camp it reduces the available riding time without a thousand kids running around. I ride for pleasure and for the thrill of spending time in my favorite place. I have plenty of kids at home.

More than that, I missed a week's lesson because my daughter was sick with a fever. It would have been bad parenting to bring her to the barn, spread germs, and sit miserably for two hours while I rode. I was tempted, but I chose parenting over barn time.

So not only had I not ridden for two weeks, but I worked that day. We had five equine massage appointments in 89 degree F weather, which really took a lot out of me.

I was not setting myself up for success.

.   .   .

Dehydration

Working all day in the heat I made the mistake of not drinking enough water, a recurring problem. For all that the researchers say 16 glasses of water per day, those working outside in the heat should definitely add to that.

How many glasses of water did I drink? Good question, perhaps two maximum. I basically survived the day on Coca-Cola.

Panic Attack

Okay, so we've established I wasn't in the best physical shape. I really wanted to see Delight and catch up with my friend and trainer, Robin, so I was determined to go. I never considered bailing. That being said, I was not motivated to actually get on a horse and exercise.

. . .

*J*ust before heading to the barn I had a serious panic attack. I haven't had one in years, but it wasn't about riding. My summers are insanity. Too much to do, balancing work, house, husband, kids, and of course, social pursuits.

I really needed "me" time doing what I love.

I applied cannabis and vetiver essential oils to my pulse points to relieve anxiety. I am a huge proponent of essential oils and use aromatherapy daily in my massage practice.

*W*ithin a few moments and several deep inhalations, my heart rate was back to normal and I could breathe again. Sadly, the urge to vomit took a while to recede.

*M*otivation

. . .

Sometimes I am not motivated to ride. Strength of will is sometimes hard to come by. I made it to the barn, three kids in tow, and proceeded to tack up Delight in a sweltering barn. It's hideous but real life; when you spend time with animals you must brave the elements.

I did tell my trainer that I wasn't feeling well and why, and so she kept checking in with me and gave me a lot of breaks for water and to catch my breath.

We worked on transitions and two-point in a forward, collected trot in a frame. My trainer asked if I wanted to do a canter, but my face was so red and I was so overheated as such that I decided to play it safe. Still I kept riding without pushing my limits too far.

That being said, Delight started to anticipate the canter because he is used to doing things in a particular order, one of the reasons I love to switch things up on him every once in a while. I don't want him to anticipate; I want him to listen.

.   .   .

*A*fterward we had a lovely walk where he stretched his neck nice and low. He even gave a few pops when turning to release tension.

*C*ooling Off

*A*ll equestrians know that you don't ride and then walk away. It was warm out and Delight worked hard. Despite my discomfort due to dehydration, Delight needed a bath and I confess that I enjoyed the cool down as well.

A Nice Surprise

*W*hile I grazed Delight, I had the nicest gift! My husband surprised us at the barn! He'd never met Delight before, and you all know how I feel about my favorite OTTB.

.   .   .

*S*QUEE!!

I can't say what impression Delight made with his intent grazing and mouth full of grass, but Jason came with us while I put on his fly mask and put him out in the paddock. He even held him for me while I went to grab something from the barn.

I definitely had a long, exhausting day. But in the end, spending time at the barn with Delight, and then introducing him to my husband, really made things so much better. I'm really glad that I pushed through and rode anyway. Cheers to drinking more water for next time.

*D*o you sometimes struggle with motivation? Do you push through or make an excuse?

24

BIG HORSES RESULT IN BIG FALLS

*C*onfession: we all fall from time to time.

We, all of us, are afraid to fail. Whether we are afraid to fail ourselves or others, it doesn't really matter. This fear can be paralyzing in its strength and create huge amounts of self-doubt.

Do you ever feel like you can't get anything right some days or even weeks? Maybe it's this looming solar eclipse, I don't know. After days of technological chaos, I was excited to ride Delight. We had a fun lesson last week when I got out of my own way, and the weather was proving to be overcast. So much better than the glaring sunshine we've recently had.

Unfortunately, things started off on the wrong foot. Delight was a total grump during tacking. Every once in a while, he shows attitude when he sees the saddle. Even when already tacked, Delight would see someone walking with a saddle and become grouchy in anticipation.

But this was a horse of another color. I went to put on his saddle pad and he pinned his ears. He then simultaneously tried to kick and bite me. Not one to back down easily from a tantrum, I kept taking the pad on and off until he stood nicely, and then I let him be for a while. The saddle upped the ante and he started to pop up on the cross ties, enough that I thought he might break them and warned my kids out of the barn.

I pulled out the big guns, peppermint.

Although not a professional horse trainer, I do know enough not reward bad behavior. I asked one of the barn girls to stand in front crinkling the wrapper to distract him.

Ears suddenly came forward followed by a curious nose, and I added the saddle and girth with barely a tail swish. All sorted. Because he stood nicely, he got the peppermint. I don't believe in holding grudges.

Delight can be cranky, but this was not normal behavior for him. I talked to his owner and we thought this was maybe because he'd been in his stall all day and was feeling pent up, or the camp kids were teasing him again, (he hates attention in his stall). Who knows? But something was off.

I thought the big lug might benefit from some lunging before our lesson but didn't push the issue because we were already running behind and my riding partner was waiting for us. It took a lot of time and patience to tack him. Besides, once the bridle was on Delight calmed down and started dozing as per usual.

During our lesson we worked on walk/trot transitions in the outdoor ring using ground pole grids in a figure-8 pattern, which was a lot of fun.

Everything was fine until we cantered.

A few things I know about Delight:

- As a Kentucky-bred OTTB he is stronger tracking left. So, I chose this direction to start because he is better at getting his lead.
- Delight has downhill conformation. I have to sit up, shoulders back, and let him have his head at the canter because his neck is naturally long and low. This helps him to balance his weight appropriately.
- He slows on the corners, especially going uphill. There was a time not long ago where we could just not get the canter in that ring and kept breaking stride.

- He likes to kick out when throwing a temper tantrum. His tantrums are rare and usually for good reason. He is predictable in what he will not put up with.
- Temper tantrums are usually caused by too much leg on his sensitive left side or using the crop incorrectly, for example on his hindquarters instead of his shoulder.

We started the canter tracking left going slightly downhill and really opened up on the long side in anticipation of the uphill turn.

I made a mistake. Instead of sitting up and driving him off my leg, I collapsed my body and flicked the crop, which was a big mistake. The normally small kick, (for a 16.2 hand Thoroughbred), became a full-fledged buck. I almost regained my seat but because I wasn't balanced in the saddle, I flew off. Picture Superman flying the air but without grace. I hit the ground HARD.

First thought that goes through my mind when I fall?
Avoid the hooves.

Despite riding this horse for almost two years, I've never fallen off him before. I didn't know if he'd bolt or stop. I couldn't move away and trusted my trainer to protect me. But he had stopped immediately, surprised I was no longer astride. The next thing I know, I'm face down in the dirt trying to breathe and take stock of my body.

I heard the crack when I hit the dirt and knew I'd hurt my ribs. I was afraid to breathe, but I did eventually. Robin sat there, kneeling next to me, with a contrite Delight poking his head over her shoulder checking on me. I would have laughed if I could, he was so cute. I was injured and absolutely covered in dirt from head to toe. I even made an impression in the hard ground.

I was in so much pain I couldn't cry, nor was I shaking from the adrenaline. I had an audience, and they got me talking. Wait, did I mention my kids were there? My kids seeing me on the ground was the icing on the cake. I had to get up and wipe myself off after removing the five inches of dirt that had embedded itself in my field boots.

My kids' reaction was a little unexpected. Rather than tears and worry the girls asked, "Mom, can I have gum?" I kid you not. Barn kids, right? Thankfully they were completely unfazed even though I wanted to visit the emergency room.

I finally stood up with help and tried to breathe. Then with a little help from my trainer, I got back on. It wasn't pretty. My ribs were definitely bruised, and I looked like a sack of potatoes. I walked around on

Delight a little while on the buckle. When we passed the impression I made in the dirt, he stopped and sniffed it curiously.

Yes, that was me on the ground.

It wasn't the horse's fault. I should have trusted my instincts and lunged him beforehand. I also should have had a better leg and better seat, but mistakes happen.

I went to the emergency room for a scan of my ribs. The prognosis was good with only three weeks off...I was very lucky.

Rather than being afraid to ride again, I was disappointed.

Who would have thought it?

25

GETTING BACK IN THE SADDLE

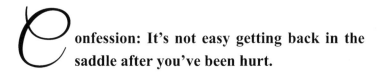onfession: **It's not easy getting back in the saddle after you've been hurt.**

Who could blame me for being rigid in the saddle after three weeks bed rest due to severely bruised ribs? I don't. I landed ribs first on the packed earth coming around a corner. WHAM! That will teach me to be too far forward coming uphill at the canter. I'm still cleaning the dirt out of my field boots.

After endless weeks of anti-inflammatory essential oils, medication, ice packs, and sleeping upright, I finally made it back to the barn! I experienced zero anxiety, which for me was a miracle. This was the first time I'd ever really been injured in a fall. And let's be honest, I'm getting older and I don't bounce back like I used to do.

I was extremely proud of myself because coming back to the barn I experienced only excitement! Lifting my saddle was a bit interesting, especially onto a handsomely tall Thoroughbred. If I thought he would miss me and show me some nice manners while being saddled, well I hoped for too much. Still, he was his best possible self. Stomping feet, ears pinned, and a tail swishing me in the face in case I didn't get the point. It was going to be business as usual.

What can I say? I'm a glutton for a sassy horse.

What I did not expect was the serious lack of grace on my part. It had only been three weeks out of the saddle but it felt like a lifetime. I was seriously out of shape. Even mounting up was interesting with my right side still healing.

I underestimated how much I actually do on a daily basis between riding and providing sports massage to my horse and dog clients. During my time out of the saddle it was like my body forgot how to sit properly. I felt completely unbalanced.

All in all, the first ride back wasn't too bad. Simple walk, trot transitions and figure 8's. Delight can be a bit pokey and trying to get him to move off my leg was a lot of work for me. I was sweating after only a few moments. I know I need to give myself a break and give myself some time to get back into the swing of things.

After all, I'm still sore and do not have the capacity to canter as yet with Delight. He's on his forehand a lot as it is and needs lifting, especially in the corners. All things considered we did pretty good the first ride back.

I missed giving Delight an after workout bath and hand graze, so it was lovely to catch up in the sunset.

Sadly, I'm also about five pounds heavier, tighter through my hips and thighs, and very tense. Perhaps I could do with a good lunging myself.

Treadmill, here I come! Maybe.

26

THE PERILS OF NOT OWNING YOUR OWN HORSE

*C*onfession: I crave something that may never happen.

Not owning a horse is a huge problem for me. This may sound elitist, but if you've been following my story you know that this is something I've been working toward my entire life.

My husband likes to point out all the perils of owning a horse. What if they get hurt, what if they get sick, what if we go on vacation, lose our jobs, etc. But what I would like to talk about is the perils of NOT owning your own horse.

Time

Barn time is real.

I own a business that allows me to make my own hours and massage horses and dogs. Win-win, right? So, I spend a lot of time at the barn. I go there to say hello to friends, human and otherwise, to massage clients, to take photos, and to take lessons. I'm there all the time anyway. I might as well have my own horse. If I have time off to myself, that leaves me to go shopping or something equally expensive. Yes, I have a spending problem. Having a horse is actually safer for my bank account as it will keep me out of trouble. For my fellow equestrians or other shopaholics, are you buying any of this? Neither did my husband.

Wouldn't it be better, and more cost effective too, to spend time bonding with my horse? Doing groundwork, practicing what I've been working on in lessons, and getting more exercise?

The Tack Situation

When you don't own your own horse there are two options.

Option One: Borrow Tack

You use the barn's saddle pads, half pads, and girths, clean or not, damp from previous rides or not. You have to remember which saddle fits you best and pray you picked the right one so you don't have to go through cinching the girth all over again. Then you have to adjust the stirrups because any number of people have used this saddle since you rode last. Chances are that no matter how well you eyeball those leathers, you're going to have to adjust them when mounted anyway. Then you need to remember which bridle fits your lesson horse, and pray that no one adjusted it for another pony, or borrowed it for a horse show and never took it out of their trailer.

Option Two: Buy Tack

Like many others, you get tired of borrowing tack. So I went the other direction. Remember? I have a problem. I own a halter, four saddles, multiple girths, half pads, saddle pads, crops, and helmets. Don't even get me started on riding clothing! And I don't own a horse…it is pretty sad. But I've made my peace with it. This is called wishful thinking…or as my husband would say, "Obsessive."

Space & Storage

My "tack room" is in a corner of the garage.

When you don't own a horse, you have to lug all your tack, (see Option Two above), to the barn. Often, I leave it in the car, and I don't have room for groceries, or the kids backpacks, etc. I do have priorities. When you don't own your own horse, you don't get to store a tack box at the barn or use a tack room. I have all the tack, but no place to put it. So I use my garage and car instead. Yes, I would rather keep it at the barn.

Think of the Children

There is nothing so amazing as watching your children enjoy the same passions.

There are so many benefits to growing up around animals and I love that my children have the opportunity. They may decide against it in future and they may come back to it as an adult like I did. It's their choice. But not having a horse of our own means paying for four people to lesson at the barn rate. The lessons are less expensive if you own a horse, but you also get more opportunities to ride, practice, and build confidence so you are getting more for your money.

The Worst Part

Finally, the worst part about not owning your own horse. The horse that you love? The same one that accepts your bad days and challenges you to be a better, more confident rider, and forgives you when you aren't? The horse that makes you laugh because he is so crabby, predictable, or just downright silly? The horse that you tell your secrets, troubles, and hopes too? The horse you didn't know you needed?

That may be the very same horse that could be sold at any time. That, my friends, is the biggest peril of not owning your own horse.

27

AMBITION

*C*onfession: **I am ambitious in life.**

Ambition is a tricky word. I consider myself extremely ambitious but only with certain aspects of my life, like my business and my writing. I have big plans and goals to which I am working toward every day. I am always working to improve myself and have the utmost confidence in my abilities. But why then, do I struggle with riding ambition?

Confidence is a problem that I've struggled with my entire equestrian life. It ebbs and flows, and I let a lot of outside influences affect how I feel. One day I'm flying on air because my horse and I are in perfect sync. We are doing everything right. The following week I feel like I've never ridden before. I'm tense, awkward, and in my own head wondering why.

Consistency

The inconsistency in my confidence depends largely on how I feel that day. Tired and stiff or alternatively happy and focused. The thing is, I can absolutely feel when I'm off. While I appreciate my trainer's comments, and they are always helpful, I know in my bones when I'm having an off day.

I've found it very helpful to set small goals for myself. Coming back from injuring my ribs in August, I had a plan. Baby steps to regain my strength and endurance, then cantering other horses before cantering Delight again. He is very sensitive and if I'm tense, then he will be tense as well. My plan worked wonderfully, and it was a success! Thank goodness I have a trainer who knows exactly what I need, although I know she gets frustrated with me at times. Then, Delight and I had an amazing lesson. We worked on transitions, ground poles, and collected canter, and we rocked it all! My elation was palpable.

I spent that weekend missing him, excited to ride again, and talking about him non-stop at the Equus Film Festival. Yes, I love him and his sassy attitude. The following Monday dawned crisp and cold, and I couldn't wait to get to the barn. I was tired, and my back was stiff, but I was so looking forward to my lesson.

It did not go as planned. We were just not syncing up due to my tension. He tried everything to listen and perform, but I was just not focused, it felt messy and I became frustrated. I made myself relax and we did exercises that kept us changing direction to loosen up.

I was disappointed in myself. Why the huge difference between one day and the next?

Because we don't live in a bubble. How we feel on any given day affects how we ride.

How we feel on any given day affects how we ride.

When I ask the question, what is my riding ambition? The answer is simply this, *consistency*.

- I want to consistently have confidence and relaxation in my riding
- I want to consistently communicate clearly with my horse
- I want to consistently improve my confidence in the saddle

This is my riding ambition and my goal for improvement.

I don't need to win ribbons to be happy, although I love cheering on my daughters at their horse shows. The trouble is that without a horse of my own my riding is limited. Less time in the saddle means less time together to play, train, and practice.

What is your ambition? What are you doing to achieve it?

28

TEN REASONS TO OWN YOUR OWN HORSE

*C*onfession: my dream has always been to own my own horse.

*I*t's true! After years of begging, pleading, and crying – I am buying a horse! Horse ownership has always been my goal. It's easy to blame my husband or finances, but the truth is that I wasn't ready before now between kids, building my business, and managing my time.

*B*ut now it's here! While I search for my unicorn, these are the 10 reasons why I'm excited to be a new horse owner. Can you relate to any?

. . .

10. Practice, Practice, Practice

Riding once per week, occasionally twice, does not allow for a lot of growth in my riding. Sometimes I chafe at the fact that I cannot practice what I've worked on in a lesson or take the pressure off and just enjoy some time in the saddle without a plan. I can spend more time in my favorite place while doing my favorite thing.

9. Groundwork

When you lesson or lease a horse, groundwork is often overlooked or not included. I've noticed that we often concentrate on exercises under saddle rather than groundwork, which is an important part of trust and respect. Horsemanship is not just in the saddle.

According to horsemanship trainer, Lorie Duff, "Groundwork is key to having a successful partnership with your horse in all situations. Handling your horse during grooming, taking extra time with them in their field or stalls, whatever the case may be. The more time you handle your horse and communicate to them a clear understanding, you will have all that benefit from a good foundation of horsemanship."

. . .

8. Building a Relationship

I've been riding lesson horses my entire riding career, multiple horses over many, many years that I've loved and learned from. Sometimes both if I was lucky. My most recent and greatest love until now is Delight. While technically my trainer's horse and not a lesson horse, I felt pride that I was one of a few allowed to ride him. Our relationship has had its ups and downs but over two years we have built a connection. I love that and I love him. But he's not my horse. While my trainer has been gracious to "share" him with me a little and often finding humor in it, there are limitations.

*W*ith my own horse I can build a relationship of trust, and hopefully affection, over time. Mine to love unequivocally.

7. Freedom

When you own your own horse, the onus is on you for exercise, health, and more. As a mother of three, dog mom to two, and owner of two businesses, I do not flee from responsibility. In fact, I relish it. I love the idea of being responsible for my horse and having the freedom to choose what exercises to do that day, under saddle or on the ground, and how often I ride. Taking lessons means limited rides per week that are susceptible to change depending on the trainer's schedule or the weather. With horse ownership, I can lesson of course, but also choose when I want to ride. I have the freedom.

6. Financial Benefits

Does this sound like a joke? It's all about perspective. Rather than spending money on dinners out and contributing to weight gain, you can spend all your money on a horse. (Also to include veterinary bills, board, lessons, and tack). Luckily, I have a head start with my amateur tack room, but there are a few things I'll be needing, like a tack box. Luckily, I'll be able to move my things to the barn and finally use the official tack room.

5. Expand the Family

This goes two ways. Unless you are a professional equestrian, and even then, your animals can become a part of your family. You are responsible for their health, happiness, and (hopefully) want what is best for them. But more than that, you become part of a barn family. The best barns are those that you can be yourself, that you trust with your horse, and that you enjoy being around.

I've been lucky to be at my barn for about six years now and can't imagine ever leaving. I've lessoned, been a working student, and done turnout and feedings as well as provided sports massage for many of the horses. I genuinely love being there with the people and feel comfortable as if I was home.

I've known the kids running around and my children are growing up there. This will only be better having my own horse and spending even more time in my happy place

4. Bring Joy to my Children

This does not apply to everyone, of course. How many of you have loved horses since you were small children? Me, me, me! My children are no different. They've trekked through snow, mud, and high heat while I've ridden or worked at the barn. They've cleaned tack, fed hay, and swept the aisles. They also all ride. Does it make sense for all four of us to spend money on lessons, or to fully commit and have a family horse that I can ride at my level, and they can grow up on?

I think every child should grow up around horses if possible. It teaches responsibility, hard work, confidence, and humility. But more, it brings them joy. We are blessed to give our children this gift. A gift they have to work hard for every day, but a gift, nonetheless. I'm finally achieving a childhood dream, and I am still in disbelief.

3. Have Fun

I have a lot of bucket list items related to horses, including riding on the beach and participating in a hunter pace. Without my own horse my chances were severely limited. I see my friends going on trail rides without me, but I'm limited as to what horses are available and at the mercy of their owners.

*J*ust think of all the things you can do when you own your own horse.

•Trail rides

•Beach rides

•Halloween costume contests

•Rodeo

•Hunter paces

•Holiday parades

•Playing in the paddock

•Just spending time together

*A*nd so much more....

2. Gain Confidence

Confidence has been my biggest issue when it comes to riding. I know we are all extremely hard on ourselves and expect a lot. I'm no different. A lot of my confidence issues stem from not being able to ride through mistakes or practice at my whim. Will my confidence increase? Perhaps...stay tuned to find out!

1. But First, a Photo

You get to unapologetically take a thousand photos

and videos of your horse without remorse! You may annoy your friends, but as an equestrian writer, it's basically my job. Get ready because this is going to be fun. Who doesn't love sharing photos of their pets on social media?

PART III

MOVING FORWARD

29

KEEP MOVING FORWARD

While horses are obviously my passion, they can even teach non-equestrians a lesson or two. The most important lesson I've learned is this:

As prey animals, horses have a tendency to turn and run at the very hint of adversity. Their instinct is to flee. As we work with horses, we train them to use the "thinking" side of their brains. Trainers tell us this all the time.

A horse that hesitates to move forward is a horse that is feeling scared, dull, or even uninspired. They can be dangerous and often cause frustration to those around them.

Is that how you want to live? Or do you want to be the

bold, curious horse that, despite uncertainty, moves forward to try new things and trusts that it is in his best interests?

It's a wonderful metaphor for life. Because things happen. Life gives us obstacles. Every single one of us must learn to either avoid those obstacles or overcome them. We have that choice.

As I was completing this book, something in my life occurred to remind me of this very thing. My massage business, my partnership, and my friendship dissolved.

My dreams for a future with my partner and our vision of helping animals through massage therapy disappeared before my eyes and rather suddenly. I had envisioned a full-time career working hands-on with horses and dogs while writing to fill the gaps and bring attention to our business. But that wasn't the reality. Starting a business and having the drive and patience to keep pushing even when things are slow, or not going as expected, is extremely difficult. We've all heard the clichés about working with friends. I don't believe it is true for everyone, but it certainly changed our friendship and created a dynamic that did not benefit either of us.

It is enough to break my heart and a business was not more important than the people in my life. But what could I do? Should I stop dreaming of helping animals?

Should I stop using the certification I received and pretend all the hard work we've done over the previous years was for nothing? It is not in me to do that. I, too, have to keep moving forward both in the saddle and in my life.

I need to learn how to move forward as well.

After wrapping up the details of my former business, I decided to start again but this time under my own name. My blog, Bridle & Bone, was hosted on my former business website with which I had to cut ties and truly start again. Now I am rebranding rather appropriately as, "The Timid Rider."

A fresh start!

Taking that first step to start riding again, to start a new business, and to write that first blog post in 2016 was incredibly hard for me. However, instead of succumbing to my fears and insecurities like I did as a child, I am now determined to become stronger and face my challenges head on.

I continue to challenge myself every single day. Sharing this book and my innermost fears and secret thoughts is terrifying, but I'm proud of myself for pushing through that fear.

I am now doing what I love – working with horses and

writing. I have room for improvement, of course, but don't we all?

Others have noticed my passion and strength, and I now write regularly for a number of equestrian publications as a freelance writer. I attended Jersey Fresh International and the Longines Masters as a member of the media and attended the Equus Film Festival as an author. These amazing opportunities would never have come my way if I hadn't stepped outside of my comfort zone.

It's scary but exhilarating all at once!

30

LET YOUR PASSION BE GREATER THAN YOUR FEAR

Truly, I am lucky. As a mother, my greatest fear riding horses is injury and the reason I call myself a "Timid Rider." I don't take chances because my family depends on me. However, this is also part of working with animals. All equestrians fall off. It's just a matter of time.

The fact is, I've never before been seriously injured horse riding before hurting my ribs. A few bumps and bruises over the years but nothing that had before ended in an emergency room visit.

Logically, I knew it was a simple accident. I wasn't scared to get back on or return to riding. Get back on the horse I did. But I was different. I was sore, I was tense, and I was unwilling to be as assertive with my horse as I needed to be. Without realizing it, my confidence had also taken a direct hit.

Do you ever have two sides of your brain that war with each other?

My emotion and my logic conflicted. And yet, I both knew AND felt that I was out of sync with this horse. Still, I pushed past my comfort zone for the next few months.

It didn't work.

I'm embarrassed to admit that. I was not improving or pushing myself. Now to my credit, my rides were not necessarily bad. I had good days and bad days, but my riding was lackluster. My trainer sensed my frustration as I am not subtle.

As a result, my trainer decided I should ride a different horse so I could regain my confidence and assertiveness. These horses would be confidence builders, if you will.

Riding other horses was exactly what I needed. I needed clear communication where I wasn't afraid to ask because of something that "may" happen. I am surely the biggest obstacle in my own life.

I am the biggest obstacle in my way.

I miss Delight and the challenge he provided. Logically,

I know that I rode him successfully for two years. However, our relationship changed and started to create bad habits for us both. I am excited to see how I progress as a rider now that I'm a horse owner.

I'm still learning. I'm pushing myself to become a better rider and not focusing on what I'm doing wrong, but instead what I am doing that is correct. I will keep moving forward no matter what happens.

When dreams come true you almost don't believe it. Yes, you have to work for them, and they do not always come to fruition. But often they do. Taking the initial step to leave behind a familiar career and become an entrepreneur in the equestrian industry unraveled a series of events that made my life incredibly richer. Could things have gone the other way? Yes, most small businesses fail, like my first business did. Yet the knowledge I now have, as well as the ambition and drive to pursue my desires, will only allow me to succeed as I dust myself off and try again. I have learned not to quit when I care about something.

If there's anything to learn from my story, it is this: pursue what you love. You may not be successful, but how do you know if you never try? I talked myself out of so many things because of fear of failure, that I never really tried. Writing, horse riding, even traveling to Europe after college to become an au pair were opportunities I was too afraid to take in my youth. The 'what if's' held me down. When I decided to stop caring in my 30's and pursue my passions regardless of my anxiety, I became successful. I was passionate and determined and that inspired others.

I don't regret the roundabout way that I found myself and my amazing life because of everything I learned along the way. I do wish I had found the confidence to pursue my passions long ago. With age came a greater sense of myself and who I wanted to be. How many people do you know who reinvent themselves? No matter their age or their background, life moves on and you can become the person you always knew you could be.

Face your fears and push through them however you can to follow your passion. Because the very thing you most fear is the very thing you may need to be happy.

AUTHOR'S NOTE

Thank you for picking up my book. Even more, thank you for finishing it!

My entire life I've loved two things: writing and animals. Because I was afraid of not living up to my own expectations, I stepped away from my dreams for too many years. This is the story of how I again found my passion, and what I've experienced as a result. I am still a work in progress.

Sometimes taking the long way around teaches you more about yourself than you could have dreamed. I believe that every decision I made led me to this point and gave me an experience, or the expertise, that I would need to succeed at what I love.

A lot of work goes into realizing a dream. I wouldn't be here without the support of my husband and our daughters. Their support and belief in me mean the world. And of course, I've been inspired by my friends at Lancaster Equestrian Stables in Monmouth County, New Jersey, whom always encourage me to try my best and support me when I'm too hard on myself.

Why should you read my story? Because I am you. Whether you are an equestrian, a mom, a dad, a pet parent, or someone else entirely, each of you has something about which you are passionate. Perhaps in the normal day to day grind you've forgotten what excites you or pushed it aside for a while. Perhaps you are just too afraid to fail. I've lived my life going above and beyond to do everything except what really matters to me. My own dream.

I'm not afraid to fail anymore because my passion is greater than my fear. You are reading my personal journey.

If my story inspires you, or just plain entertains you, please take a few minutes and leave a review on Amazon and tell your friends. As an independent author, I do it all on my own and reviews mean so much.

If you are interested in my future books, please follow

me on Facebook, Twitter, or on Amazon and Goodreads.

Don't forget to follow my adventures on my blog, *The Timid Rider*!

ABOUT THE AUTHOR

Heather Wallace is a Certified Equine Sports Massage Therapist (ESMT) and Certified Canine Massage Therapist (CCMT) working diligently to reveal to the world the benefits of natural therapies for animals through both hands-on work and writing in her award-winning blog, *Bridle & Bone,* now rebranded as *The Timid Rider.*

Heather is also the Content Manager and a regular writer for EquineInfoExchange.com and contributes to a number of publications including *Sidelines Magazine* and *Holistic Horse Magazine.* Her first book, *Equestrian Handbook of Excuses*, was a 2017 Literary Selection for the Equus Film Festival.

In her spare time, (of which she has little), Heather spends her time with her husband, three children, two dogs, and her new pony, Ferrous. You can follow her on social media @timidrider or at timidrider.com.

f facebook.com/timidrider

twitter.com/timidrider

instagram.com/timidrider

BOOKS BY HEATHER WALLACE

EQUESTRIAN HANDBOOK OF EXCUSES, 1ST EDITION

Girl Forward: A Tale of One Woman's Unlikely Adventure in Mongolia (Book)

Equestrian Handbook of Excuses, 2nd Edition

The Timid Rider (Blog)

Animal Massage Therapy

Animal Bodywork and Aromatherapy

Podcast

Equestrian Pulse Podcast

Follow Me:

Goodreads

Amazon Author Page

Made in United States
Troutdale, OR
01/18/2024

16996198R00113